Walter the Cowboy (Seattle, WA)

An old cowboy

Not dead yet

Upped and left

And tipped his hat

First published in Great Britain in 2025
by Kindle Direct Publishing

Copyright © Neil Bradley 2025

The moral right of the author has been asserted.

ISBN: 979-8-31179-690-3
Imprint: Independently Published

Front cover art work by Brad

For Jack, Allen, Neal and Charles.

And for all those others
beaten down by life.

With Thanks

Throughout the years of (not) writing this book, or any of my other (unpublished) books, there have been a host of people that have influenced and encouraged me, as well as offering me the kick up the backside I so very much needed to finally get it finished, despite all of them, no doubt, not being able to understand any of the poems and songs that follow.

As always, I would like to thank my, long-suffering, wife, Sharon, for her love and unflinching belief in me, especially over the last few years when it looked like I'd never write, let alone finish, another damn thing.

I'd like to thank my late father, Jim Bradley, for his love and eventual understanding.

I'd like to thank Lee the Lift for all of his attempts at encouraging me to finish this book, even though it's not actually the book I promised him.

I'd like to thank all the folks at The Long Pond, my spiritual home, for their friendship and laughter, and for buying all of those paintings.

Lastly, I'd like to thank Joe Baden for his love and friendship, and for saving me all of those years ago!

Foreword

I first spoke to Neil, what seems like a hundred years ago now, in the corridor of Goldsmiths College, University of London. Back then, he was a writer for the esteemed Millwall fanzine, *The Lion Roars* with a body of work running into the hundreds of thousands of words and I, a fellow devotee, although much lazier follower of the South East London religion. A few years earlier, I had founded a fledgling Higher Education project and he was working in the International Admissions Department.

My opening gambit of, "S'cuse me, mate, can I have a word!?" was received by Neil with a distinct look of suspicion, a look to which I was soon to become accustomed. Goldsmiths Open Book, I told him ran a weekly Creative Writing class, and as you are a writer, do you want to take a session? Again, the look of suspicion this time merged with incredulity. Since that distant day though, I have seen Neil grow from a reluctant tutor to an accomplished novelist, podcaster, artist, songsmith, poet and educator. Throughout our relationship one thing has never changed, he still thinks me a spiv and I think him, far too Bohemian. But we are forever, brothers in arms!

Our paths in life exhibited incredible parallels and massive divergencies. We are the same age, were brought up in and around the same area, of South East London, had many friends, family and people in common, never went to our respective secondary schools on a regular basis, both went into the printing industry aged 16ish, are of the old industrial left, both chronically miserable, and even have our own respective Sharon's as our wives. There however, the similarities end; Neil took an honest honourable path to working drudgery and me a very different path to the same end. That is until we found learning and the closest we can ever come to serenity.

Before I met Neil, my understanding of the mechanics of poetry was vague at best, a haiku was what Irene Handl considered an indication of intelligence; I didn't know my sonnets from my acrostics! Sitting in on Neil's classes and observing his students evolve from writing limericks, into budding bards is nothing less than epic, if you excuse the pun. Neil's progress from writing the odd elegy to becoming an accomplished poet and songwriter, has been no less dramatic.

Neil's work is representative of most of us at Goldsmiths Open Book, cynical, working class, sharp, sometimes hilarious, often tragic, but always human. This, his latest publication will take you on a journey through the world according to Brad, a paradox world of colour and monochrome, humanity and spite, cynicism and hope. The anthology is in many ways, a wry historiography of the angst that many baby boomers have suffered, trying to negotiate the transition from the twentieth to the twenty-first century. Neil relates through his work how being 'afflicted with poetry' can ease the pain but never truly cure it; and God forbid it ever does. For it is from such confusion and misery that great art grows!

From the irritation and, may I say, horror, of rail replacement services to train travel during Covid. From the working-class, day to day, stereotyping based on accent and annoyance towards an entitled culture that refuses to recognise the struggles that created the freedoms we have today, the Camberwell boy's beatnik alter ego, Brad, screams relentlessly from the inside of his head. This body of work does not come from a bourgeois soul, searching for gritty realism and pretentious middle- class academic acclaim, but from a working-class heart whose beat resonates with the genuine masses and is real; Neil is a genuine artist!

On a personal note, I couldn't ask for a better friend, though I'm not anywhere near so spiritual or artistic, we are both kindred spirits, and very much Goldsmiths' answer to Tony Hancock and Sidney James!

Joe Baden OBE
Director and Founder of Open Book
Goldsmiths, University of London

Kitchen Sink Dharma

(Poetry and Songs)

By

Neil Bradley

FOR NICK
WITH MUCH LOVE
+ POETRY!

BRAD

x

Poetry Please

I remember during my Master's degree in Creative and Life Writing at Goldsmith's College sitting in a writing workshop where we had just read a piece of text from a novel, and the tutor asking whether any of us had spotted the author's 'little joke', which he'd hidden in the text, and to which everybody else in the room began nodding and giving collective knowing laughs. I, on the other hand, just sat there, blank-faced, and definitely not getting the joke.

"Well?" the tutor prompted.

"It's a sonnet," someone eagerly proclaimed, and with everyone else nodding in agreement – all of them thinking it marvellous.

Not wanting to appear ignorant, of course, I smiled along with everyone else, even though I'd not got the joke and wouldn't have recognised a sonnet if it had walked up and slapped me around the face.

When I was at school – a terrifying example of everything that was wrong with the British Comprehensive education system – I can't recall doing much poetry, and even when we did not one of us was ever brave enough to embrace it with any real enthusiasm. Besides, as I'd told the Admission's Tutor at Goldsmith's when I met for my interview to study for an MA in Creative and Life Writing, you could get beaten up for listening to David Bowie at my school, so the likelihood of enjoying poetry was definitely out of the question. And yet, those poems were actually no different in their way to the lyrics David Bowie had written – lyrics that I'd memorise each and every line, and which I could recite on demand like a performing Diamond Dog. But then, I didn't realise that back then, during those torturous school years, and I certainly didn't realise that fact when I was 'faking it' in those creative writing workshops.

Whenever we had to 'workshop' our fellow students work I would always be full of dread, especially when it came to submissions of poetry, none of which I understood, even though I was always complementary, as I was with all of the submissions from my fellow students, regardless of the genre, which I thank came down to the fact that I'd most certainly not come from an English Literature background, but which had most certainly been the case with regards the majority of those I'd studied with. Indeed, I'd not done a first degree, despite my writing for many years and having a giant portfolio of work that I'd written, and was only really doing my Masters on the recommendation of Joe Baden, who was the Founder and Director of

Open Book at Goldsmith's, and with whom I'd been volunteering for the previous year or so. And, of course, it wasn't just the poetry criticism that I always had a problem with. To be honest, any such demand of me to critique a fellow student's work filled me with similar dread, not feeling qualified as a result of my poor education to make any comment whatsoever, whether I liked it or not – this was especially true of the stuff I didn't like, which I'd always be over-complimentary about, even more so than the stuff I did like, and which I think comes from my upbringing, which, despite being somewhat challenging, lent itself very much to being polite always and never offering criticism of any kind, especially criticism of another's creative efforts, in case it offends.

Of course, I know that doesn't help when you are part-studying literary criticism, but it's most definitely something I've never quite managed to conquer. Besides which, I always felt that I'd never had enough experience of other writing forms - poetry certainly – and therefore felt that I was simply not qualified to offer up any criticism whatsoever. Even on the odd occasion when we were required to write something in a poetic form, as part of a weekly writing exercise session, I was always completely self-conscious, usually delivering something flippant, as is my writing nature, or something cringe-worthy in the extreme, something poncey in every measure, stuff I'd immediately destroy with a vow never to write poetry again.

Not that I fully gave up on poetry or, more importantly, the poetry 'scene'. Amongst many of the wonderful people I met during my studies – people I wouldn't have met under any other circumstances – there were a whole host of poets, all of whom appeared really committed to their craft, despite my lack of understanding of what it was they were both doing or attempting to achieve: with novelists it's easy, in the same way it is with life writers (which I now most definitely consider myself to be). With us there seems to be an end goal, that we're creating something immediate and tangible, which is not meant as a slight on the poets. One thing I always admired about the poets though, indeed was envious of them in many ways, was there sense of community and their unwavering commitment to share their own work and the work of their fellow others, with poetry readings taking place every single night, all of which were given and received, I was to discover, with a genuine sense of generosity, which I've not always found to be the case with more formal and structured writers. Of course, it's far easier to get up and read a handful of poems, especially for the audience, than it is for a novelist or a life writer to deliver long chapters of the books they're working on, so it's little wonder that there are fewer reading opportunities for us. Even so, I always found this world most welcoming,

9

and there was very much a sense of community, which every writer needs, even if the actual production of the craft itself always takes place in isolation.

And so, I often found myself attending these poetry evenings, which on the whole I enjoyed, but which still never filled me with any real confidence that I could ever write poetry myself. That is until Covid-19 came along, followed by the Lockdown, when I suddenly found myself at home with time on my hands: my wife, poor cow, worked throughout the pandemic, so never got to experience that sense of freedom and isolation that I did, despite my timetable quickly filling up with the delivery of on-line classes and over-long, over-compensatory meetings on TEAMS or ZOOM, although none of which, initially, tended to interfere with my sense of being stuck on some desert island somewhere.

It was during those first few weeks of the pandemic, prior to the Lockdown, when there seemed to be a genuine fear amongst the majority of us, that I needed to perhaps make sense of this new unknown – before this new 'normal' that we all became part of – and that I suddenly felt an overwhelming need to capture, in writing, some sense of what was both going on in the world at large and the way I was feeling personally. And then one night I suddenly sat down and wrote the first poem I'd ever really written in anger – a poem that I didn't flinch at the writing or reciting of – which I was suddenly happy to share with friends and family and with work colleagues, and which, I always thought, captured perfectly that sense of what was going on in the world. And whilst that first poem was nowhere near perfect, it was very much typical of my writing style in all of its flippant glory, and most definitely gave me the confidence to write more, which is very much the point of this book: if I can write poetry; if I can write songs (which are reproduced in the second part of this book), then anyone can, surely?

Poetry

All poems in this book are written by Neil Bradley

Covid-19

(the first poem I ever wrote)

How did things get so bad

In these best years

The best we've ever had

Apparently

Distant news at first

It'll soon be in reverse

We're always told

Like wives' tales of old

But no not this one

The one to end all

Say some

A cough

A fever

From some old geezer

Who you've never met before

Clearing his throat

Spitting on the floor

And now we're not at work

Have we got it

Who can tell

Can't get to see the doctor

He's too unwell

Told to stay at home

Lay on the floor

A cross painted on the front door

Call one-one-one

And so begins the fun

And games

The old

The lame

They'll be the first to get it

And then it will be us

And then they'll be an awful fuss

Who's to blame

What to do

Have we got enough paper for the loo

But don't panic, eh

Keep calm and carry on

Living life in the same old way

But there's panic everywhere

Clearing the supermarket shelves

Wondering what to wear

Grabbing pasta

And handwash

And giant packs of toilet paper

They're even stealing handwash

From the hospitals now

So there's bound to be an awful row

These people they could care less

No wonder the country's in such a mess

Stay at home

By yourself

Let the world go mad

It's just a passing fad

We're told

Only affects the old

Your mum

Your dad

Peak out through your curtains

At all of the others

Uncertain

Like the zombie apocalypse

And not a single tourist

At the acropolis

Italy in lockdown

Spain is in a state

Germany thought of invading Poland

But they'd already locked the gate

Get yourself a hobby

Learn to paint

Or play the piano

Beat yourself again

At Scrabble

Hang spring cleaning

Hang yourself

Read all of those unread books

Sat upon the shelf

Take an on-line course

Sing until your voice is hoarse

Anything to beat

Defeat

The boredom

Anything to beat

The blues

Maybe sort out all those shoes

You never wear

In this time of such despair

We know it isn't fair

But them's the brokes

So come on, folks

Cheer up

Embrace it

Self-isolate

Elevate

Put your feet up

Turn it into something

Cultural

Something

Not so guttural

Something to end

On a positive note

Before they demand

You get your coat

As you sit and smoke

That last cigarette

Dunk that last biscuit

In that last drop of tea

Think about what might have been

Had none of us

This virus ever seen

When all was bliss

Just one long kiss

Instead of your last

These final days

Are all I ask

Be kind to yourself

Be kind to others

Cuddle the dog

Kiss your wife

Tell them how much you love them

How much you love life

Turn off the television

And the radio

Draw back the curtains

Wide

Have a bit of pride

Wave to your neighbour

Do yourself a favour

Fall into a trance

Play some David Bowie

But not let's dance

The Woman on Zoom

I fell in love with a woman on Zoom
sat there smiling in a different house
the meeting arranged in separate rooms
with her children, a dog, a cat, and spouse

the boss gave her a right old dressing down
which I thought was cruel and unfair
coming to a meeting in a dressing gown
contemplating a nice virtual affair

bet he's got vodka in his coffee cup
but he doesn't see you the way I do
only professional from the top half up
doesn't see you as I see you

she sits there in her kitchen
as I the dining room
wonder what she'll be cooking
come the afternoon

i thought she looked nice and told her twice
something about work was the pretext
i said so again, which now made it thrice
sent her a message, said so in a text

and then this morning I saw her husband
come in from the sitting room
and caught a glimpse of children
one or maybe two

and that had my heart sinking
yet thought there was still a chance

do you love me, i was thinking
please tell me with a glance

but she looked off blankly
frozen off in time
it upset me quite frankly
that she would not be mine

buffering me with silence
without no reasoned rhyme
buffering me with silence
towards my love decline

A Look

A man gave me a look the other day
A look that said, I don't like you
Or people of your type
Even though he didn't know me
Even though he didn't know anything about me
Contemplating that man's look
I thought I'd give him a similar look back
But then suddenly thought better of it
Thought that maybe he was unhappy
Unhappy with his lot
Unhappy with his life
Unhappy with his dog
Unhappy with his wife
Unhappy with his job
Unhappy with his past
Unhappy with his prospects for the future
Poor sod.
Looking at me like that

I'll give you a slap, you mug

The Harbour Wall

I went for a walk last week
At the coast
Near the sea
Quite near the harbour wall
Across the road from a fairground
That no longer welcomes all
The town is dead the locals say
Especially from September
Right through to end of may
And even then
When the sun shines
In June, July and August
Still no one comes
Except me
Escaping from it all
Walking alone
quite near the harbour wall

San Francisco Revolution

Oh, San Francisco
Will Russian Hill invade North Beach
Will the townsfolk Howl
Will the proletariat
Be storming the Palaces of Fine Art
Will the new administration offer free cable
Are they truly on a Mission
Or simply off their trolleys
The establishment quakes

At the thought of reviving Castro

Standing on the shoulders of Giants

Faking Chaplin in City Lights

Sheriff forms a Posey

Oh, for the Harvey Milk of human kindness

It can't be right

It can't be right

That people like me

Happy-go-lucky

Free spirit that I am

Should be pegged back

By the nay-sayers

The negative brigade

Those people that

Can't see beauty in a sunset

Or a badly-painted landscape

Or freshly-toasted hot cross buns

Those people that insist on moaning

Or pouring scorn

Spoiling it for others

Upsetting the apple cart

Upsetting the quiet of the day

With some bullshit or other

It's Written

To wonder at stars

To wander beneath their memories

The distant echo of their spark

Deceitful in their glow

Their shimmering light

A remnant of their past

There Are People Like Me

there are people like me
and there are people not
those that question everything
and those that do not
those that are cynics
and those ignorant in bliss
those that long for kisses
and those that just kiss

there are people like me
long in the tooth
those that get depressed
at clouds above the roof
those that want sleep
an escape from it all
those that want an end to this
a permanent nothing at all

there are people like me
melancholy to the last
people like me
that yearn for the past
there are people like me
that wander alone
that draw all the curtains
and switch off the phone

there are people like me
not many it's true

that daydream their days
in skylines of blue
there are people like me
that run with the wind
that long for the days of dying
and then die in the end

there are people like me
that are still young at heart
that mourn for those
that they've witnessed depart
that have left this world
left us behind
that we considered friends
that were caring and kind

there are people like me
and there are those that are not
but I won't throw my hat in
with any of that lot
the bullies, the takers
the greedy, the mean
and people like me
who just want to scream

so, here it is . . . merry christmas (acrostic poem)

so one hears echo repeated echos
in towns
in suburbs
mechanically engineered
robin redbreasts
yearning christmas harp renditions
in sad tradition

marketed as slade

The Alphabet (acrostic poem)

acrostic bohemian came down each Friday
gregariously hatted
insinuating jargon
killing lonely, mean nonconformists
oppressive police
quelling riotous, surly teenagers
ugly, visceral, wild xanadu-yearning zeniths

8-Line Poem using 8 of the above words

a **bohemian** chap
gregariously dressed
jaunty **hatted**
lonely sometimes
especially on **friday**
when he became **wild**
and then came **down**
from his **yearning**

Words for a Poem

what words should one choose for a poem?
words that consume
words that create juxtaposition
words that cause division
between those that love
and those that desire heaven above
those that die too late to be saved
to find grace
those that curse the human race

its frailties

and its vanities

and its vagaries

its odds and sods

and boring jobs

and days of regret

and sure-fire bets

to which they never staked claim

instead blew it all on fame

and fortune

and non-realistic dreams

that couldn't possibly come true

of lost loves

and impossible loves

and loves that passed them by

loves that die in the blink of an eye

with no one to mourn their loss

the loves you choose

the loves you lose

the loves you lost

to fate

or indifference

or to someone with a better skillset

someone who's a safer bet

someone you wish they'd never met

like they met you

that love once true

a love to end all others

like those in films

like those in songs

like those in books

those to which we long

those which so long ago departed

without goodbye

without farewell
lost to spells
like some distant star
that disappeared a million years ago
yet which we still see
up there in the galaxy
through a telescope of the heart

Sonnet the Hedgehog

a hedgehog shed skin in fields where I walk
he left it there upon the grass one day
found a job in London was the talk
left a note for the milkman, gone away

said he'd had enough of the nine to five
he packed it all in, said, that's my lot
on such meagre earnings could not survive
packed his little suitcase and off he trot

lives in Camden with others of his set
looks back, finds his life profound
the most exotic creatures met
got a job on the London Underground

lives in the shadows now, avoids bright lights
sweeps up dead human skin and hair, works nights

The Virus (part 1)

There was a virus came to town
Here and to other places
All around the world, they said
A virus spread by love

A virus spread by friendly greeting
By way of a kiss
By way of a handshake
By way of a hug
By way of a friendly embrace

No one knew how the virus started
Was it from a single kiss?
Was it from a handshake?
Was it from a hug or friendly embrace?

Keep your distance, they told us
Don't go where other people are
Avoid crowds
Avoid schools
Avoid work
Which I've attempted doing my entire life

Wash your hands thoroughly
For twenty seconds at the very least
Whilst singing Happy Birthday to yourself
Even though it's not

Jacob Reece-Mogg
A time traveler from the past
Suggested singing the National Anthem
Whilst washing your hands
But I've always been a republican
A fervent anti-monarchist
So that won't do
Besides, I always sit that one out
Which can be awkward
When washing your hands

So that's the advice

A twenty-second handwash

Which sounds like something you might get

At a massage parlor of dubious curtains

No happy ending for anyone

A Virus (part 2)

on the train

a man sneezed

and everyone held their breath

a woman coughed

and eyed her suspiciously

another woman wiped her feverish brow

and everyone changed seats

The Virus (Part 3)

I got on the train this morning

absolutely packed

not a seat to be had

so I coughed dryly

i wiped my feverish brow

i rang my wife and whispered loudly,

"i think I've got the virus!"

suddenly the carriage cleared

numerous seats became available

so I sat down

four seats to myself

enjoyed my journey

in peace, comfort and quiet

Arkansas River

6th longest river in America

Flowing through Little Rock

Clinton had his card marked

Unable to pass bill after Bill

I did not have sexual relations with that woman

until they came upon the dress he came upon

Claiming it a dress he simply came upon

Dan's search for love

There was once a man

A strange man called Dan

Who lost love to maidens

Long ago forsaken

Women of a certain age

Once all the rage

Those of poor virtuous soul

Who, down boulevards, stroll

But, poor Dan, without sophistication

on another ride is taken

And left penniless and alone

No love to call his own

A man in need of a violent shove

A man who only wanted love

But life is not so generous

And Dan's life horrendous

So much at love he tried

Until, finally, he broke down and cried

His life well and truly over

Never to be spent in clover

Crime Number

all meetings these days
must have a cheeseboard and wine
not that the metropolitan police
will investigate the crime
certainly not in retrospect
which means my dad
has no chance of his burglar
being caught
despite the crime number
and a letter informing him
we're sorry you've been a victim
of said crime

Describe your current state of wellbeing in 30 lines
(a writing exercise for an Open Book Creative Writing Class during the Lockdown)

i'm like Peter Finch in 'network'
I'm as mad as hell
and I'm not gonna' take it anymore
okay, so I exaggerate somewhat
most days I'm just cold
especially in the morning
my bones ache
i feel older today
than i was yesterday
a whole year has gone
in self-isolation
even when i'm not alone
with no end in sight
with no good news
other than a vaccine
that doesn't seem to work

beyond the sell-by date

despite matt hancock's reassurance

you'll just feel a small prick

i need a holiday

in one of those empty hotels

in London

locked in

tracked and traced

my every memory

I wish I had never started

Binge-watching

game of thrones

winter is coming

An Old Cowboy

I met this old cowboy
In a bar one starry night
A long way from the prairie
His eyes they twinkled bright

Me and You

if I were you
and you were me
would you see the you that's me?
or I the you that's you?

The Lost Husband

I met a woman today
whilst enjoying coffee
on the high street
who had lost her husband

on previous occasions
whilst enjoying coffee
on the high street
her husband had been with her

Today though
Whilst enjoying coffee
On the high street
Her husband was nowhere to be seen

"I've lost him," she told me
Whilst enjoying coffee
On the high street
"I've lost my husband."

"I'm so sorry," I said
Whilst enjoying coffee
On the high street
"Had he been unwell?"

"He's not dead," she said
Whilst enjoying coffee
On the high street
"He's lost."

"Lost?" I said
Whilst enjoying coffee
On the high street
"When did you last see him?"

"He was in a photo," she said
Whilst enjoying coffee
On the high street

"Above the fireplace."

"Our wedding day," she said
Whilst enjoying coffee
On the high street
"Forty years ago."

"Now he's lost?" I said
Whilst enjoying coffee
On the high street
"Nowhere to be found?"

"First, he lost his head," she said
Whilst enjoying coffee
On the high street
"And his memory with it."

"Then his legs gave," she said
Whilst enjoying coffee
On the high street
"Followed by the rest of him."

"If they were to take a picture now," she said
Whilst enjoying coffee
On the high street
"I would be standing alone."

Why Can't I?

Why can't I be like everyone else?
Why can't I just let it go?
Why can't I walk without a care?
Why can't I stop to the smell the flowers?
Why can't I be satisfied with my lot?

Why can't I be satisfied sat watching the telly-box?

Why can't I not just think so much?

Why can't I stop being so angry?

Why can't I stop being so frustrated?

Why can't I stop being so troubled by the world?

Why can't I stop worrying so much?

Why can't I just stop?

The Marriage

They'd tried everything

Talking to family and friends

Talking to each other

Relate. Marriage Guidance

to those of an older disposition

They'd tried being all 'touchy-feely'

They'd tried couple's retreats

They'd tried date nights

They'd tried extreme sports

They'd tried gardening

They'd tried badminton

They'd tried yoga

For which they bought

themselves matching mats

They'd joined a choir

Him a deep baritone

Her a diminutive alto

Yet they never managed

achieving harmony

Then one day she'd come home early

From her job in the library

Only to find him

Made up like a geisha

Wearing her favourite frock

Fluttering feathers

posing in a mirror

where their eyes met

Across a spick-and-span bedroom

"What do you think?" he'd asked.

"I'm not sure," she'd replied, "although I think you've gone a little slapdash with the rouge."

"Do you think so?"

"Here, let me show you," she smiled for the first time in such an oh, so, long time.

With one hand she applied another lipstick mouth upon him

Whilst he squeezed her other hand

Telling her

"Everything will be alright."

After that they both rushed home from work each new day.

Eager to make-up

Dress up

Perform their little cabaret

For the benefit of the wardrobe

And the dressing table

And the velvet curtains

And the flock wallpaper

More in love now

Than they'd ever been before

Like two, heavily-made-up, birds

Of a feather boa

Three Stupid Monkeys

There is a view that:

You can't unsee what you've seen

You can't unhear what you've heard

You can't unspeak what you've said

And so you are:

Burdened to the point of sadness

Burdened to the point of madness

Burdened to the point of misery

Burdened to the point of insanity

Burdened to the point of no return

My advice:

Forget your troubles

Forget what you've heard

Forget what you've done

Forget what you've seen

Turn on the radio

And dance

In the kitchen

All Four Walls of the Office Where I Write

Tommy Steele

Smoking a fag

Peggy Mount

Smoking a fag

The Dude Lebowski

The Dude abides

Debbie Harry

Playboy Bunny

Paul Weller

Changing Man

Heather Graham

With fake cockney accent

David Bowie
Of course

Citizen Kane
Rosebud

Johnny Cash
Sun Studios
A $250,000 picture

Kimono My House
Nicholas De Ville
Coolest man in London
Sparking Ron and Russell Mael

Some painted Harlot
What's her name?
Virginia Plain
Nicholas De Ville
Coolest man in London

Edith Piaf
In the darkest corner of the room
Covering up the damp patch:

MASH
Suicide is painless

Tony Hancock (The lad himself)
Nick drake
Ian Curtis
Elliott Smith

Billy McKenzie

Virginia Woolf

Hunter S. Thompson

Ernest Hemingway

Marilyn Monroe

The Proclaimers

Glasses

The two Ronnies

Richard Hell

The voidoids

Love comes in spurts

Blank generation

I'm leavin'

I'm gone

Slade

Thumbs up

Dr Feelgood

Oil city confidential

Levee's gonna' break

Thames Delta Blues

Buster Keaton

Silence

Buster Bloodvessel

Lip up fatty

Buster Merryfield

During the war

Del, Rodney and Granddad

Lovely Jubbly

John and Yoko
Tackle out
Two virgins

Brian Eno
In roxy music
With hair
Before leaving
For some faraway beach

Medication time
Jack the dulled boy

Edward munch
Scream
A knock-off
Yours truly

Dean martin
Drinking green river
Oh, it's boozin' time

Lichtenstein
Pow!

Kenneth Williams
Carrying on

The 'Family'
Bournemouth

George Harrison
My Sweet George

Brian Epstein
Poker dot scarf
Ray Bans

Super, Super Neil
Happy 40th

A bout de souffle
Jean Seberg
Leaving me breathless

Penny and vince
Despite the terrible news
Just good friends

Dear john
Any sexual problems?

Bryan Ferry
To Neil
Bryan Ferry

Mods

Neil Young
Harvest Moon
Shining on the wrong side
Of the house

Barney Sloane
Turning off the windscreen wipers
In the snow
Crashing the car

Just one of those things

The London Marathon

Wonder women

Super men

Hiawatha

Rupert the Bear

A deep-sea diver

Women in tutus

Men in tutus

Men in drag

Women dressed as Charlie Chaplin

Runners on stilts

Runners on jelly legs

Runners carrying canoes

Runners running for the sake of it

Runners running for charity

Save the Whales

Save the Children

RSPCA

Fight Cancer

Fight Strokes

Fight Dementia

Fight Alzheimer's

Fight the good fight

Christian Aid

Food Aid

Water Aid

Water Station

A million discarded water bottles

Save the Environment

37 Darth Vader's

All claiming to be my father

Tony Bennett

Oh, the good life
Tony Bennett
Fixing his gaze on mine
Stood between two television cameras

Oh, the good life
Tony Bennett
Fixing his gaze on mine
Stood between two paintings

Oh, the good life
Tony Bennett
Fixing his gaze on mine
Stood between two framed photographs

Oh, the good life
To Neil
With all good wishes
Tony Bennett

Inflicted with poetry

The news has broke
"Poor chap," they all say

He's been inflicted with poetry
Last year it was photography

"Haiku," I cry
"Bless you," they reply

Crash, bang, wallop
Trollope

"Ted Hughes," I cry, for no apparent reason.
As the feminists line up to cry, "Treason."

"Ted Hughes," I cry.
Then watch another poet die.

Shall I compare thee to a summer's day
No, thy shall not, go away.

As if I have any say in the matter.
Attempting words that flatter.

Byron, Keats, Shelley
Digging at the underbelly

What is my life?

What is the meaning of life?
Can the secret be chanced upon?
Can it be found in an extra hour in bed?
Or in the smile of a woman on the bus?
Or at the sight of sun breaking through cloud?
Or in a break in April showers?
Or in an April shower itself?
Or in the gentle falling blossom from trees?
Or in the discovery of a ten-pound note in the street?
Or in a silhouetted girl's striptease?
Or in kicking through fallen leaves?
Or in the smugness of a new haircut
Or in the escape of a recent rut
Or in having Friday on my mind?

Or in hiding behind the blind?

Or in waving to the neighbour's dog?

Or in the freshly burning smell of log?

Or in the Turner like gaze of skies?

Or in the love in a mother's eyes?

Or in the wagging tail of a dog

Or in the breaking through the fog?

Or the electric shock of fingers upon your neck

Or in the warm body lying next to you in the bed?

Or in the cheery good morning of your work colleague, Fred.

A train into London

As the train crawls

Slowly towards childhood

Memories of London

Bridge falling down

Drunk, immortal youth

Care free and care less

Screaming at the world

Go hang, go hang

Portraits of the artists

As younger men

Statue like

Unknown

Soldiers

Entombed

In bronze

Uniforms of khaki

Taking the king's shilling

And marching off

To war, to war

To war with you all

Ignoring the historic

Shadows of our past

Destiny

Reborn

In wine bars

In bistros

In coffee

Emporiums

Of the caffeine

Soul searching

Clues

In cross words

Puzzling

Over cryptic

Verse

Going down the tube

Closer to eight

Than midnight

Like ants

In ant hills

Escalating tension

Among unattractive tourists

In search of crop

Circle lines

And Bobbie's on beats

And horseradish

Source of England

Glorious

Empire State

Of confusion

In vauxhall

With reigning queens

and Bill's bloody plays

Of kings in winter

Getting the hump

With discontent

Being taken for a ride

On the bakerloo

to Waterloo

Changing there

Into Wellington boots

To splash water

On the queens

Jubilee line

Living the life

Of the damned

Refusing to get off

At West Ham

The seventh

Circle line

Of hell

Blackheath Village Blues

An ambience of wealth pervades

Traffic fumes

Around the one-way system

Disguising itself

as fragrance

Women of a certain age

Looking as old as they should

Their troubles far less

Than mine

Or disguised better

Beneath tasteful pearls

And swirls

Of grey-blond

Curly hair

The academics
And the art pandemics
The scholarly
The well read
Mahogany-bedded
Dreams of Empire
In the shadow of a church spire
Built to an English God
To whom they feign belief
Yet give credence to
Urban mythology
Black Plague Londoners
Buried beneath
Well-drained sod
And the tramp, tramp, tramp
Of hunting dog

The unhappy home

There was once
an unhappy home
With moping wallpaper
And a sulking staircase
Its rooms cold
And damp
And frankly
inhospitable

In the water tank
In the loft
Floated a dead pigeon
Its heart stopped
And slates missing
From its roof

And the garden
Beyond the kitchen door
Sat overgrown and unloved

Along the passage
Going back in time
The threadbare carpet
Disguising cold stone
And in the scullery
Sad appliances
Long since loved
And mice abandon all hope

In the kitchen sink
Drama
No meals have been cooked
Or prepared with love
No kettle boiled
On troubled water
Engaging flame
With North Sea Gas

Upon the stairs
Every third one creaked
And the thirteenth one creeped
Wincing with each step
As though in pain
Like a doormat wife
Walked all over
All her married life

In the living room
Velvet exotic birds
Flock from the wallpaper

Swarming around

The damp patch

Above the mantlepiece

And the ticking clock

Long since lost its tock

The rail replacement bus

A fitting end to a week

in London

that started with me in despair

and ended here

Hell on earth

Outside the station

My fragile existence

In the balance

Left in the incapable hands

Of a rail franchise

That runs no trains

Certainly not on time

Certainly not on my line

When all I want to do

Is to go home

To go to bed

To rest my aching head

Creeping age

No longer

All the rage

Inside me

My only hope of escape

Leaving too late

To save me

The Girl Outside

Outside I found you smoking there
Sat there on that battered chair
You looked at me with eyes so bright
I asked you if you had a light

And then we danced the night away
Then danced into the next of days
Not thinking 'bout the love to come
Not thinking how let it be done

Caught your smile beneath the neon light
Never seen one shine so bright
Dancing 'neath the whisky sign
My love for you I was resigned

But now we've danced for far too long
Still dancing to that same tired song
Too old to let me change the tune
Too young to let it bother you

So that song it does another round
And we dance to stop us falling down
Come too far to turn back now
Too proud to finally take a bow

Time to Share

Once upon a timeshare
A man with dyed blond hair
And speedo's
And a sixteen-inch choker chain
For an eighteen-inch neck

Bragged he'd got it made

With his big-breasted wife

Number two

Called Denise

Lived happily ever after eight

Minted

Until he went skint

And she traded him in

For an older model

With better prospects

And a larger portfolio

A cafe down the road.

There's a new cafe down the road

Where I went one day

To write

Only to have my creative stumblings

Drowned out by hungry grumblings

Of yummy mummies

With yoga-flat tummies

In sunglasses and uggly boots

Proclaiming their genius children

With their colouring books

Congratulating themselves

On the success of their private viola lessons

And the books they boast on their shelves

And the hiring of a personal tutor

"He's a deputy head, you know."

All coming in from the rain

Ignoring my disdain

Coveting each other's husbands

Highlighting their perfect lives

their perfect hair

Their pretensions

Coveting each other's loft extensions

Ignoring my disdain

Ignoring the John and Yoko

Yearning from the table opposite

Never once realizing

I'm only trying to get me some piece

To finish this poem

In quietus solitude

Of contemplation

Away from the brattish demands

Of eggs Benedictus

And dinosaur toast

Over indulged to the point

Of young conservatism

Ignoring my disdain

And yet still

The decibel levels rise

Drifting up the walls

To paintings in frames

For sale

Local artist

The park at dusk

In acrylic paint

We trust

And then the rain comes

The alfresco mother's

Running for the covers

Scrambling for inside tables

And eggs

And the best vantage point

To spy traffic wardens

Throwing up cordons

On the prowl

Here they come

The mummies howl

Their derision

Cursing the local council

And their restrictions

Ignoring my disdain

Not feeling my pain

Full of doubt

I want to scream

To shout

All the right words I write

Not necessarily in the right order

Previewed by Andre

Who serves me coffee

With a sympathetic smile

Before returning to the tea urn

An earnest young man

Who's putting himself

Through veterinary school

No dogs, sorry

The man greeted at the door

Who's been before

Who knows the score

With forlorn pooch

And a hankering for tea

Even though he gets none

And little sympathy

Andre pointing to the sign

On the door

And the dog bowl

Half filled with water

And a jar of doggy treats

Whilst the man and his dog

Stand with sodden feet

Let me pull out the awning

The man yawning

Along with his dog

To whom he gives a nod

To protect you from the rain

Which he promises will stop

As if upon the command

Of a clock

So soonest mended

The man

And the dog

Befriended

Ignoring my disdain

A new place

For me to write

To contemplate

Something new

Words

For you

My writer's pain

Seeps from indiscreet speakers

Where Leonard Bernstein

Struggles to make himself

heard above the facile din

Orchestrating his chagrin

Whilst I sing along

Inside my head

When you're a Jet

you're a Jet all the way

I'll proudly boast

To my last dying day

As the mummies screech

Like banshees

Ignoring my disdain

Ignoring the fact

That I wish to get away

Not once, ever

Taking a breath

or realising

I Want to be in Americano

Rob

Rob always entered the room

Unannounced

Never centre of attention

Always smiling wryly

And looking

A little perplexed

With Rob

There was never a lot of fuss

No histrionics

No sudden outbursts

World-weary

To the point of dreams

Pulling out his little notebook

Full of graphic secrets

And wonderful verse

Of which he was never quite sure

Everything gentle

Everything Understated

Funny and Insightful

With accompanying drawings

Never once revealed

A man of few words

On paper.

Love in the Launderette

Remember when we made love

In the launderette

Keeping our whites white

Separating the colours

Removing our underwear

Pulling the wool over prying eyes

Ignoring the warning signs

Dry clean only

Tumbling, tumbling, tumbling

Making love to the beat of a drum

Cursing our detergent lives

Lived beneath neon signs

And a woman demanding change

Comforted by comfort

Yes, sir, yes, sir

Three bags full

The Fat(ish) Woman

There was a fat(ish) woman

She was always smiling

Though she never ran

Or skipped

In case she slipped, I suppose

into a coma

Got to live her life over

A thinner life

Of healthy eating

Or putting in appearances at the gym

At the yoga classes

In yoga pants

Wearing sunglasses

And drinking pick champaign

Never one to complain

All love is vain

Features plain

Never skipping

Worried about tripping

Worrying about someone

Evening, Brad

The guy behind the bar calls me 'Brad,'

And I call him, "Mate."

I think his name's Kevin,

but it could be Blake, for all I know

But then, my name's not Brad.

And I'm not sure how he's come to such conclusions.

But I continue to call him Mate

And he continues to call me Brad

which cements the friendship

which cements the illusion

A Mother's Love (Affair)

My mother fell in love

With the man that delivered coal

Each week she'd watch him from above

From her bedroom windowed vantage lull

Standing tall, black and soot tan
My mother thought him such a very handsome man
A man to whom she so very much desired
Who called weekly when the coal expired

This man who captured her heart
This man who came each Tuesday
Arriving each week upon his cart
This man who made her heart woozy

And then one day this love turned to lust
Having lured him towards her slack hole
My dad caught her black handed with coal dust
To where she demanded he pour his coal

My dad put an end to it though
Told the man he needn't oughta
Told the coal man where to stick his coal
Cancelling all further orders

Sadly, it didn't stop her wandering eye
Regardless that they'd changed supply
Her desire turned to the electric man
Who turns up occasionally in his electric van

Soon enough, sparks flew between them
Another one of these utility men
Who came to read her kilowatts
Told her he loved her lots and lots

Who lured her one day beneath the stairs
who made her forget her worldly cares
Until dad came home early once again
Berating my mother for her sin

And now all love is lost to her desire

Which started with a roaring fire

It's that makes mum's passion stir

So if you see Sid, tell him

I Fell, I Fell

You were too playful

And I too drunk

And too unfaithful

Under normal circumstance

I should have slunk

Curse my happenstance

Away, away

so far away

From your loving arms

And your siren charms

Determined not to fall

Into your deepest pools

Immediately disarming

Even if alarming

Of blue chlorinated water

Like lamb to slaughter

Even though I shouldn't oughta

Dive in the shallow end

Happy to be alive

Happy to survive

My time with you

With you

With playful you

Entwined we two

Lost in you

With you

In loves embrace

A mysterious case

Where heart break detectives

Find me defective

Guilty as charged

Water

so we beat on, boats against the current

borne back ceaselessly into the past.

days through weeks

months through years

an outpouring of grief-stricken tears

seeping below the water table and chairs

a veil of tears, pouring, pouring

across linoleum flooring

breaching flood warning defences

over garden fences

engulfing fields of dreams

and swelling streams

with no outlet for its torrent

a knocked over bottle

of Yves Saint Laurent

and roads by any name

could smell so sweet

praying for the summer heat

to mop and sponge away

the water, water

get me to the alter

and point me in the direction

of some new path

to make me laugh

again

The Hypochondriac

Have you heard about Old Bill
He's only gone and died
What, Bill from the bakery
Who makes the Mother's pride

He was a martyr to his ailments
Said Mary down the pub
I felt sorry for him, she said
He was always on the vapo-rub

Bleedin' hypochondriac
Proclaimed her husband Joe
He was always standing at the bar
Telling tales of woe

Remember that time with his chesty cough
Complaining about his shin splints
Sore feet, and runny nose
And an allergy to mint

He took himself to the doctor
At least once or twice a week
And around the doctor's door
He sheepishly would peak

What on earth's wrong with you this week
The doctor would bemoan
Please stop coming here so often
Just call me on the phone

But Bill was having none of it
I've paid my National Health

And all those other taxes
I've given up by stealth

I need help with this funny shoulder
I need your help real quick
I need you to take a look at it
Is it something you can fix

He felt bilious one day
Taken from the latin
I'm bilious he told the doctor
Who prescribed him angiostatin

I used to take it all in stride, he said
But now I'm stiff
Each morning when I wake
All down one side of the bed

He once caught hypochondria
From a drafty room
And never wrote a single postcard
After catching dyslexia on his honeymoon

His wife she never loved him
No woman ever could
Especially once she caught him
Beneath the cooker hood

He claimed he was lighting the grill
But she knew that was a lie
She has the image still
Because there was nothing in to fry

And because he had no matches

And the windows were bolted shut
A draught excluder up against the kitchen door
And the poor canary in its cage dead upon the floor

I'm leaving you, she told him
And off she went to pack
And he thought for a moment about pleading
But there was no turning back

And after that, he simply sat
And worried about his health
He worried about his itching legs
And these peculiar red welts

That appeared all over his body
And some upon the floor
He was going to call out to his wife
But she'd already slammed the door

And so he was left alone
With too much time to think
His throat swollen like a blocked drain
Just like the kitchen sink

And after that, it happened
His ailments getting worse
Pins and needles in his hands
Each new symptom now a curse

Landscaping the garden one day
He caught pea shingle
You should've heard him groan
And for weeks after that
He had trouble passing stones

I'm going to pot
He called to his wife
But she'd left years ago
So heading off towards the shed
he sat there all alone

The next thing to go was his memory
Although that wasn't very long
Hearing on the radio
A long-forgotten song

And one day he misremembered
Having Covid number 4
Then remembered that was his old house
The one with the red painted door

Insomnia kept him awake at night
So depressed did he become
Counting sheep through lack of sleep
He counted every single one

And then he woke up stiff one day
To match his once stiff back
Lying there in a parlour state
Like being tortured on the rack

Of course, he thought he'd live for ever
Like most hypochondriacs do
but it's usually one of us that dies
And it's never bleedin' you

But then one day without warning
Right out of clear blue skies

The hypochondriac woke up to find

He'd only gone and died

And just like poor old Spike Milligan

There was no turning back for Bill

And upon his headstone was inscribed

I told you I was ill

Reliant Robin

Consider the robin

Reliant in winter

With its rust red breast

And its AA membership

Digging through frozen ground

For eighty worms per day

And no overtime

Brit Poem

These days

I don't see much

From this one eye

An occasional bird

As it flies by

And other park life

In the green wonderwall

Down the end of the garden

All of it a blur now

An oasis of Britpop

In this place called albion

The Barking Dog

A dog sits in the window

Watching the world go by

Every now and then he barks

Howling at the sky

They should shut that dog up

Say the neighbours

Next door down but one

But that dog likes barking

It's his way of having fun

Voice of an angel (Tube Station)

my accent is bad

At least to some

It's rough and coarse

And really isn't done

In places where they speak nice

All proper and correct

Places to which an invite

I'll never likely get

But it's the same accent as my dad

And his dad before that

And my mums was pretty similar

And so's my uncle pat's

An accent worth hearing

Despite the missing vowels

A voice of the people

A voice that never fails

To raise up in anger

At our collective lot

To scream out of injustice

And a losing of the plot

So think twice before

You criticise

'cos you haven't thought it through

It's the only voice I've got, you see

So, g'on, fuck you

Good morning

Waking up begins with saying

Good morning world

Good morning wife

Good morning dog

Good morning dressing gown

Good morning hall

At the top of the stairs

Good morning staircase leading down

Good morning hall

At the bottom of the stairs

Good morning dining room

Good morning kitchen

Good morning kettle

Tea, if you please

Good morning back door

Good morning well used lock

Good morning garden

Good morning sun

Good morning dew

Good morning robin

Good morning grass

Good morning world

again

Coffee House Blue

I see you those days you're blue
Sat across the café from you
Your bruised arm and that blackeye too
Wondering just who did that to you

Those blue eyes of yours
Put me in a spin
Even when they've been crying
I guess that's one of those love things
That you see in movies sometime
Or hear about in a song
When I'm anxious
Just to see you
Not sure where I belong
In the story

And you smile at me across the room
A guilty smile midst the coffee house gloom
Your secret out, at least to me
My coffee drained, your cold tea

And those days I wish you'd stop awhile
Reveal the you behind the smile
Stop a while and speak to me
About this love turned misery

Why would you want to be with him
When you could be with me
Some piss artist's muse
You know you have the right to choose
Your fate
To leave

To stay

Just knock it on the head

Either way

Don't fall for his drunken charms

Don't fall back into his arms

Those brutish arms of his

Longing for one tender kiss

That never comes

Because you know it means nothing

At least not to him

His love for you

Wafer thin

His broken promise

To which you cling

And yet, you think your life

will be saved somehow

That things will change

Although you don't know how

But it doesn't work like that

And you took too long

To consider the fact

Of things

Those awful things

That awful truth

That god-awful truth

Those things

You hoped in youth

Would visit you in later life

Like some movie line

Some celluloid lie

No happy endings

Depending on the wish you make

Or upon some list you make

Of some better life

Sometime soon

Thinking soon enough

Really can't come soon enough

Monday on my Mind

Monday comes but once a week

But comes around too often

Tuesday's pretty much the same

But the dread I feel softens

Wednesday's not as bad

If it hadn't been for Monday

And Thursday's not all bad again

If it hadn't been for Tuesday

Come Friday I can breath again

With the weekend one day away

But usually that gets spoiled

What with thinking again about Monday

Those Women

They're quite loud

To me

Their conversations boring

To me

They have nothing in common

With me

But one of them smiles

At me

Even so, they're not

For me

They're respective lives irrelevant

To me

But they're sitting there

Right next to me

And I can't explain why

It's so annoying

to me

The Shabby Man

There's a man in our street

I see him most days

He's never stopped to speak

Although I remember once he waved

He looks a rather shabby man

His coat's seen better days

His hat is pretty crumpled

He seems very set in his ways

A neighbour told me one time

He used to have a wife

He thought perhaps she'd left him

Or, worse ways, that she died

He thought his name was Albert

But he couldn't swear for sure

Lived in that shabby house

The one with the shabby door

He said he was a quiet man

Kept very much to himself

But had sent him once a Christmas card

Which he'd put upon the shelf

Something about the picture
A lonely festive scene
Some shabby man with brolly
Walking a snowy lane

He said the man in the picture
Reminded him of him
The way he walked our street
That shabby man, who waved once
But never did again.

Blue Clouds

One day I'll go to heaven
Get some peace for myself
Laugh at those blue clouds
Much better than here

The Rescue Dog

He might be only small
But he's really loved so much
By the people that rescued him
Who took him on a hunch

There was something about him
Something that made them melt
Even though some of the other dogs
They all looked far more svelte

Some were graceful
Some had shaggy coats

But this little dog somehow
Stood out to them the most

So they quickly signed the papers
And counted out the fee
Took him straight home with them
And fed him his tea

And now they take him walking
Each and every day
And when the weather's really nice
They end up miles away

Because he brought them something special
Added something to their lives
Something that wasn't there before
That made them come alive

And now when they watch the telly
And the chain's upon the door
They look down at him lovingly
As he lays there on the floor

In My Head

In my head I look like Steve McQueen
Or De Niro from that Taxi Driving scene
Stood in front of that mirror
Or driving those mean streets
Talking to himself
Are you talking to me?

Other times I am a pop star
Like Cosmic Dancer Marc

Especially when my muscles flex
Born to boogie in the dark

Or even Maurice Mickelwhite
In Alfie Elkins role
The only south London boy I know
Who's not been on the dole

Or Terry and Julie Christie
Outside the underground
Then crossing over Waterloo Bridge
Far from the madding crowd

Frank Bullitt from that San Francisco scene
On the corner Clay and Taylor
The coolest man in all the world
Stealing that newspaper

All The World's a Stage

My life is filled with drama
It's tragic so to speak
And if all my world's a stage
I'll close within a week!

Another Shabby Man

He seems pretty lonely
If only at a glance
One of those stand-offish types
I'd probably advance

He seems to meet nobody
I've never heard him talk

I just see him sometimes
When I'm out on a walk

Not sure if he works somewhere
Or doesn't have a job
He might be unemployed
Like me, that time, poor sod

I've rarely seen him smile
Or whistle a happy tune
Just passes by me slowly
The very picture of doom

I often wonder somehow
What's going through his head
Is he thinking about a woman
Or is he thinking about his bed

But then maybe he's an angel
Whose breathed his one last breath
Or maybe it's worse than that
Maybe he's death

The Woman on the Bus

The other day
Upon a bus
A woman looked at me
A smile of recognition
Upon her face I see
From another life perhaps
Or someone from my past
Someone I was once in love with
Some love I thought would last

Longer than my bus stop past

And suddenly she shapes

As if to talk to me

And I wait with bated breath

And whatever it was she were to ask

I would certainly have said yes

But then she seemed to change her mind

Said not a single word

And then stood and rang the bell

Any chance of love absurd

I Can't Stand the Rain

I hate it when it rains

Especially when it's wet

On those days it rains

I get as far from it

As I can get

A weather report can make me weep

Especially if predicting rain

Falling down my street

On those days I tend to stay at home

Go back to bleedin' bed

Because I like being dry much more

Than I do being wet

There's something depressing about the rain

All that water running down the drain

Seeping up through my shoes and socks

And when it rains, I'll often take stock

Usually about my life and such

The futile things I do

My relationship sometimes
The love I have for you

That time when we first kissed perhaps
Beneath that blazing sun
I think perhaps it was that day
When that raining stuff begun

But what if it had rained that day
Would that have changed our fate
Would I still have kissed you
Or asked you on that second date

Coffee Mornings

I sit most mornings in Marks' café
Writing in my little book
Poetry or a song perhaps
But mostly just the this and that

Around me are people of a certain age
All arriving at the same time
Usually about half-past-nine
All of them out on the town
Flashing all that silver pound

That'll be me soon, I often think
As some old boy gives me the wink
What, you got no work today
Or what, another holiday?

But then he has no concept of my life
Wouldn't understand the things I write
Which I capture in that little book

Not even if he took a look

Hancock's Half Hour

These days I'm feeling very Tony Hancock
Sunday afternoons at home with just that ticking clock
Bill Kerr permanently on the rock and roll
Griselda Pugh, Baby Doll

A pint, a pint, that's very nearly an armful
I'd have stood more chance at Fred's pie stall

Sat there wondering what it's all for
Should've gone with Sid on that mystery tour

And someone opened their north and south
That story they wrote in Blabbermouth

Kenneth Williams turning up in ill-fitting jacket
So I made my escape to the Hand and Racket

Nice – 8 lines

Met a couple in the coffee place today
  "How are you?" I asked
  "We've not seen you in ages," they said.
  "I was just thinking that myself," I nodded.
  "How's your dad?" they asked.
  "Oh, he's not too bad, thanks."
  "That's good."
  "How's the tortoise?"

Cheery – 4 lines

She was laughing to herself
Which made me smile
Laughing away, she was
Feeling up the produce

Joy – 2 lines

Did you see the sunset last night?
Yes. Beautiful.

Waterloo Sunset

Sunset on waterloo
Rays of sun
A song or two
Terrence and Julie
Bridging the gap
Escape the dirty old river trap
Safe and sound
Far from the madding crowd

Don't Pigeonhole Me

I'm not a faded picture on a postcard
I'm not the address written on the back
I'm not the stamp franked in foreign climes
I'm not the wishes you were here
I'm not the pen that revealed the ink
I'm not the hand that held the pen
I'm not the wrist that supports the hand
I'm not the arm attached to the wrist
I'm not the shoulder or the neck above

I'm not the head that sits atop

I'm not the brain contained within the skull

I'm not the blood vessels

I'm not the nerves

I'm not the neurons

I'm not the glial cells

I'm not the grey matter in-between

I'm not the memories retained

Yet Another Shabby Man

Walks into sunset

In his shabby coat

And his shabby hat

The shabby bloke

With his two shabby cases

Containing everything he owns

Walking alone

A lifetime in distance

His memory fading

No longer in any rush

To get to nowhere

In particular

Pictures of Lilly

Consider the Lilly

Pictures of

Who?

Remembrance Sunday

Outside spoons they stand

To pay their respects

Pints in hand

Vaping merrily as they await

The sombre tones of a cadet band

That marches past

Not quite in step

And no real understanding of their duty

To the dead and the poppy

Too young for war

Thank god

What was it for, eh?

Gallantly playing an unheard tune

That everyone's heard before

marching in ragged lines

To a drum and pipe band

On ragged remembrance Sundays

All us men that never went

Across a fractious land

In remembrance of faded photos

That hang halfway up the stairs

Upon faded walls

Great grandfathers

Great uncles

Great second cousins

Twice removed

From our memory

That never returned home

Buried in a mass grave

Beside some Belgian road

Who, had they lived to see the day

Would be dead by now

And there'd be no faded letter

In a cabinet drawer

Tell all back home I've gone away

Tell all back home I've gone to war

Poetry Blank

I've never been much for poetry
I don't understand it for a start
Or a stop
Or rules regarding the full stop
Should it rhyme
Or four-four time
Itself to death
Masking its true meaning
Or just kept squirrelled away
For a rainy day
Like this one
Today

A Morning Mood

It's difficult to put into words
The feelings I feel
Each morning
Upon awakening
With each new quashing
Of that routine nagging alarm
A new dawn
A new day
A new way
Of looking at stuff
Rather than the old
Rather than feeling old
Rather than feeling cold
Even in summer
Rather than feeling
Those same feelings of dread

Struggling out of bed
To start another day anew

Today's the day
I say to myself
Slippering downstairs
On slippered feet
The radio on
The kettle filled
The cup prepared
The day revealed
The view from the kitchen window
The same but different
As usual

I put a key in the back door
Step out into the garden
Slip into the fake wicker armchair
Sip my tea
Contemplate my fake life

Fill the kettle again
Coffee this time
Repeat the process

Run the bath
Listen to a podcast
Reluctantly shave
Dry myself

Dress myself
Prepare for a new day
The whole process
Taking much longer

Than this poem

Finally leaving the house

Catastrophe avoided

Not today

I think

Not today

Just Say No

A young man

In the chemist shop

Waits patiently

For another shot

Of methadone

Talking loudly

On the phone

With his dealer

Asks how he is

Why he's not been around

Whilst the rest of us

Hear one side of the story

Every beat of his heart

And his inner voice

Saying

Isn't it about time

We took a trip

Dulce et decorumesque

Sat writing poetry at a makeshift desk

Dulce et decorumesque

Studying an empty frame

No picture

A depiction of a family member

That no one can quite remember

No photograph ever shot

Unlike him, who was

A far distant memory loss

So come Sunday of remembrance

I will remember him

Who bore some resemblance

To me and mine

Trudging through mud and lime

Until one summer yet to come

When they plough the fields

And the iron harvest yields

The shell of that man concealed

Old war horses and the nag's head

Immortalise the glorious dead

Great Britain

Never before have so many

Owed so little

To so few

United in ungratefulness

Ignorant in their bliss

Not even a blown kiss

My arse

Unhappy Passing

I see this woman sometimes

And I often wonder why

you seem to me unhappy

The way you sometimes cry

Or often have that faraway look

In your eye

That says more about you

Than that well-born grudge

The way you're often quiet

when down the road you trudge

Covid Blues

They're talking third and fourth waves now

The men from the ministry

That earlier optimism of a vaccine cure

Crumbling like world economies

And dashing hopes

Of newly-booked holidays

At the start it was all Vera Lynn

And spirits of the blitz

And we all know how that turned out

Up the spout

All sat at home

Drinking bleach

You've been tangoed

Misguided hopes that it would all be over

By Christmas

Cancelled

Monsieur Hulot Goes Shopping

Jacques Tati

In Poundland

Walks the aisle

Pointing at stuff

With his umbrella

A pipe between his teeth

Raising his hat

To mothers with screaming kids

Wondering how much

Each item costs

Larkin About

parents fuck you up

warn you as to all of this

damn Larkin about

Sweet Una Stubbs

Our lovely Rita died today

Little Rita Garnett

Straight off the chocolate box

And that box in the corner

Of every home

with her Biba waistline

and her Sassoon poet hair

arguing till she's blue

in the red face

whilst mother looks on

all fine and dandy

and chairman Alf holds court

screaming the virtues

of Sir Winston

and her glorious majesty

arguing with Tony's father-in-law

the lazy, scouse git

delivering his Speight of the nation address

Fake News

You're better off watching none of it

I tell my dad

The BBC

The daily mail

And LBC

Which he takes all in

With his morning tea

That woman off the morning telly

Who's husband's in a coma

Jaimie fox

News and CBS

Your right to choose

Your fate

Your news

Your president

Your tan

Tiny house nation

Tiny hands

Tiny minds

Tiny tears

That other one

From the soaps

Flogging leather sofas

And life insurance

And a funeral plan

And that one off the news

Who foretells the weather

With the flicky hair

Celebrity dancing

Like she no longer cares

Anymore

About squally showers

And photographs of flowers

Sent in by a viewer

Her appearances fewer now

She's taken her final bow

Hanging up her sparkly routine

Back to the doom and gloom

Of darkened rooms

Of winter's here

With little cheer

And little prospect

Of current bun

Except in the newsagent

Bought by a man

With a hacking scandal

To go with his

hacking cough

like all those Proud boys

Too proud to wear a facemask

Or heed the warning

Or take the knee

Happy wearing pillow-cases

Over their heads

But not as facemasks

To protect them from the walking dead

Despite what agent orange said

Supressing a cough

Suppressing their voices

Suppressing their right to choose

Fifteen-minute warnings

Of pride before inevitable falls

Their cold, dead hands

Virtual hustings

And rebel yells

Crying god for harry

Meghan and boy George

The Young Bloke as an Artist

I see you some days

Through your window

When I pass by

In your artist apron

And attire

The young man as artist

In your Jackson Pollock tie

The young man not so young

Layering the lily pond

And yellow Turner sky

I spy you from afar

Like Edward Hopper

Through a blown curtain

Or the door ajar

In Rothko blue pyjamas

Or his red period dressing gown

Giving Constable

A dressing down

And on these days

I have so many questions

For you to ponder

Your tortured face askew

Questions on which for you to chew

To give answers only you would know

About the direction of travel

Your paintings go

And each time I wonder

In your studio

Where you paint at night

Contemplating brushstrokes

And the coming morning light

Fingering the canvas

Taught and tight

Still blank to the touch

Still void of life

I wonder do you dream in oil

Or pastel shades of white

Is your room aflame with orange

Or vivid red

Do you sleep in a burnt umber bed

What passes for the time of day

In your world

Does for you the nine-to-five

Even exist

When you contemplate your muse

Do you have a lunch break

And steal from them a kiss

Or is your life one long exhibition

In your head

A constant showing off

To your friends

Do orange dots on frames

Bring a smile

Another picture sold

Another hung out to dry

Or do you mourn the loss

With silent humility

Like a death in the family

Do you count the cost

It takes on your soul

The thought of another

Blank canvas hole

Tortured Poet

There is often no rhyme

Nor reason to

The poetry I write

Shifting words on lined paper

Typed up at night

Just before I go to bed

Where I lie awake and think

Of other words instead

Of the ones I wrote

Words which

When I read out loud

Catch in the throat

And choke me

Wound me

Torture me sometimes

Yet rarely set me free

Of myself

Doubt in every line

Until the sunlight shine

Of mourning

Pours through the window

And on the page

Diminishing like ink

My rage

Conspiracy Merchant

I think it's all a conspiracy

My friend said

Even though for weeks

At the start

He was sick in bed

And his mother died from it

The virus, the covid

You'll be telling me next

That a man didn't land
On the moon, I said
Even though my dad made me watch it
Got me up out of bed

Look at the picture
He said in reply
The flag points the wrong way
That's not how they fly

And then there was the second gunman
That shot JFK in the head
It's about big pharma
He continued the thread
And that Bill Gates
And his wife
Wanting us all dead
So even now
He refuses to wear a mask
Except when he's in bed
Claims you can catch it
In your dreams
From Elm Street Fred

His arguments hold no water though
They just don't make sense
They make me rage with anger
Like Jim Royle said
Conspiracy my arse
There, enough said

What lies beneath

What lies beneath

The rubble upon my desk

A diary from last year

An old Reader's Digest

To whom I once wrote

With publication hope

Of fame and fortune

Only to be greeted by stony silence

A deaf ear

No reply

Not even a thank you

For your distant correspondence

One suspects my writing

Far too dense

For those with a critical eye

Who want to be lifted

By the words of others

Lifted up and flung in the air

I tell you now

It's just not fair

And so I return to my desk

And the rubble of my life

Mourning the fact

That no one loves my words

That no one loves me

The mounting pile of unwrit words

On my desk

A paper pile slagheap of debris

The Money Trap

I walk from the station

Having escaped my mask

And my day's work

And my daily grind

Walking home

Only to find

Others going in the opposite direction

A night-time economy burden

All of us like rats

Racing to defeat

Longing for the day

When slippered feet

Greet the dawn

If we get to make it that far

To the bitter end

Retirement men

And women

With few years left to live

To enjoy the time

Those working lives

Were meant to give us back

In kind

Gently Falling Snow

I can tell snow when I see it

I can recognise rain

When it's falling outside my window

And I know I want none of it

I know I don't want it

Falling on me

Thank you very much

Without a Leg to Stand On

A one-legged man

hops through life

wondering what

it would be like

having two legs

or even one leg

twice

Government Health Warning

if you swallow the pips

an apple tree will grow

inside you

and you'll feel all scrumpy

and doomed to live

a life of cider

Please Don't Stare

please don't stare

at my shaving cut

my fraying shirt collar

my beer gut

things lately

have not been great

and that's why to parties

I'm usually late

You see my wife left me

I'm sure you heard

For a younger man

Which seems absurd

At least to me

Even though she goads me

With postcards from overseas

All signed, I'm free, I'm free

Of you

Which always hurts
Although she always did
Have a way with words
And a kitchen knife
Which cuts right through me
Slicing each new memory
Until even I forget
We were once happy

Blank Looks

I passed a woman on the street one day
Gave a little smile and a little wave
But when I saw her again the next day
she smiled not once her gaze astray
and then the day after that she crossed the road
no doubt having some other place to go
and then the day that followed
her gaze was almost hollow
fixed upon some object in the middle of the road
and I knew then I had no real chance
of a smile, a wave, a kiss
of love and romance

The Drugged-Up House

There's a house across the road
I think they're growing drugs
There's no snow on the roof
And a constant smoky fug
They're always coming and going
All hours of the night
And one day outside
There was even a fight

My dad confirmed my suspicions

He swears I tell the truth

Cos someone told him up the pub

A bloke with one tooth

swears they're druggies

He thinks the bloke's name's Fred

He's seen him up the high street

And he's got a bald head

He's got one of those tattoos he said

Which is always a give away

Until I pointed out to him

Everyone's got them today

But he was having none of it

They're druggies in that house

There's queues outside their door

And the police were there the other day

So you tell me what for

I think they're selling cannabis

They're even selling crack

They're probably selling heroin

So what do you think of that

But perhaps we're over-reacting

Perhaps there are no drugs at all

But just to be on the safe side

I'll give the old bill a call

Little Piggies

There's a bloke at work

Keeps micro pigs

Feeds them donuts

And syrup of figs

Calls them Gert and Daisy

We all think he's crazy

But he loves those pigs, I tell ya'

Shows pictures to us all

He bought them from a bloke he knows

From Istanbul

The Micro Pub

Six beers on a blackboard

From session bitter to best

From India pale ale to stout

Such volume

Omicron

It's back again

It's been on the news

Spreading like wildfire

Being Passed on and on

This one they're calling Omicron

Christmas is coming

The turkey's getting sick

There're outbreaks in Brighton

And some in Hackney Wick

But the PM assures us

Christmas will be fine

No danger of it being cancelled

Although his party's on the line

But he claims that he's not worried

And to prove this the case

He had his party last year

With Champer's by the case

This Thing

Twilight brings a wave
Sunset brings the rage
Against the dying light
Against those birds in flight

What is this thing we feel
This thing that makes us real
When all around is truly fake
All those mistakes, you know, for us to make

What is this thing called love
This thing that comes from stars above
This thing we hope might one day be
This thing involving you and me

The Bestseller

A bloke approached me in the pub
And asked about my book
And after I explained it to him
He said he'd take a look
I told him where to buy it
And what it's all about
And he promised he'd consider it
And left me in no doubt
But did he go and buy it
Did he fuck the rotter
He went straight on amazon
And bought Harry Potter

Tax Them Till They Scream

You can't take it with you
Unless you're rich
They take it with them
And claim interest on the switch
They have these accountants see
That help them cook the books
Which means that the tax man
Rarely takes a look
And as for us
If only it were so
We come into this world with nothing
And there's fuck all when we go
Because we don't have accountants
Or conservative ways
Each one of us just pays, pays, pays

Calm Before the Storm

There are moments
Not many I grant you
When everything makes sense
When the things that beset me
When the things that trouble me
Finally resolve
And briefly I feel a sense of calm
But those moments are few and far
Between
And I spend my days
Once again
Just wondering

Christmas Passed

What if we wrapped all of the presents back up
Gave them back to the people
That gifted them to us
What if we took all the decorations back down
And put them back up in the loft
What if we put all the Christmas cards
Back in their envelopes
Sealed them
And put them back in the post
Return to sender
What if we stopped thinking
About Christmas past
And simply went back there
What if we just stopped
There in the past
Would we be any better for it
Would we be any happier

A Room with a View

I looked out my window today
and saw a world outside
unchanged from yesterday
but changed all the same
the same as it will be tomorrow
the same view
the same world

Mike's Half Hour

There's a magical place
Just up the road from where I live

That serves crafted beer

From three pound sixty

To four quid

A pint

A pint?

That's very nearly an armful

Big Wednesday

Wave upon wave

Surf's up

Big Wednesday

Goofy-footing

Waxing my board

Until another variant

We Are the Mods

Once more unto the beach

Dear friend

Those summers of our discontent

When the millions like us

Descended on a bank holiday rush

Decking chairs and rockers

Without care

Anyway, anyhow, anywhere

Brighton sixty-four

The establishment mad

And wondering

What it's all for, eh

Calling us petty

little sawdust Caesars

when everyone knows

we're Diamond geezers

all mod cons

and never had it so goods

post-war Britain

well out of the woods

and now this

shattering the bliss

of peacetime

with no reason nor rhyme

the youth of today

and the local mayor

red-faced

I wished they'd stay away

Because they all need locking up

They all need their collar's felt

They all need a bit of national service

And a little bit of national health

And darling harold's

Taxing self

Ten shillings in every pound

Hit 'em where it hurts

They'll soon come round

And settle down to domestic bliss

As underneath the pier

I steal from you a kiss

Lucky jim

Time gentlemen please

I like drinking beer

It gives me a warm glow

It gives a sense of wellbeing

A sense of meaning

A sense of belonging

A sense of comradeship

With others in the pub
Them drinking too
Everyone basking
In the fake fire light
And the laughter
And the occasional song
A moment shared
In collective escape
Until the landlord calls last orders
Until the landlord calls time
Until the landlord demands to know
Have you lot got no homes to go?

Dear Sir

For years I thought about you
That game leg you had
That Frankenstein shoe

Taking that disability out on everyone
You certainly made physics no fun
At all, none whatsoever
All of us taking cover
From well-aimed chalk
Or blackboard rubber

Again, boy, that old familiar roar
What are you thick or something
No, sir, just struck with terror

I always wanted to say with glee
Yet simply just agreed
Thick, sir, me? Probably

And when it came time to administer
All those punishment beatings
To boys barely in their teens

You did so with such high zest
To any kid that mocked in jest
Or who turned on that Bunsen burner

Or all that other gas
Numbing ourselves of
That physics mass

And you with that monstrous talk
Beating us useless
With that precarious walk

The End is Nigh

I'd often see him up the high street
I can remember him from way back when
His message always the same
His sandwich board a little worse for wear
Himself a little worse for wear
The End is Nigh
"Take no notice," my dad always said. "He's a crank."
The End is Nigh
"He's been walking up and down this high street for years."
The End is Nigh
"He's still here. We're still here!"
But now he's not.
Most people think he died.
No one really knows for sure
I wonder at the end
If he realized tragic irony

That 'The End is Nigh'
Was for him
And not for us

Gary the Gas

Gary the Gas was a ladies' man
Driving round London in his plumber's van
Bibbing at the ladies, wolf-whistles too
On his way to a job in Waterloo

He liked the simple pleasures
Liked a beer or two
Sometimes liked a snort of coke
If he could get a toot or two

He had no complications
He liked the simple life
You can ask anyone
Just ask his second wife

He got stopped the other week
Which was a bit of a pain
On his way to a job he was
By that 'Just Stop Oil' brigade

He ripped the banner from their hands
Was at pains to make them understand
Cursed them to their very face
He told them, fuck the human race

I'm due at a job in Vauxhall
so I need to get there now
I'm on an emergency call

And there won't be half a row

But they just stood and smirked at him
And that had him seeing red
I'm Gary the fucking Gas, he said
I'm CORGI-bleeding-registered

The Happy Meter

Oh, the happy meter
It swings from one to ten
Sometimes it's at the top
But then plummets back again

But what I really wish for
Is something in-between
A point at which
It's not so often been

Somewhere around the number five
A perfect time to be alive
Somewhere distant in the past
But those moments they never last

Instead, it all comes back again
As it's so often been
I'm either stuck at number one
Or up at number ten

The Christmas Tree

He bought a Christmas tree this year
From a little man
Who sets up each and every year

In a big white van

They said he was the best in town
Sold each one with a Christmas carol sound
Some Slade and a little Wizard wish
And mistletoe beneath which to Christmas kiss

Well, he took it home, and he stood it up
Hung fairy lights and some twinkle stuff
Then waited till it had grown Christmas dark
Then plugged it and sparked a spark

And the memories came flooding back
Of Christmas day with mum and dad
Oh, those memories came thick and fast
Of childhood and that Christmas past

That Noise

What is it, that noise I hear
What lies behind that door ajar
From which the sound of gentle breathing comes
Like the whirling heat of a computer hum
Some sad siren call I fear
Calling me to shipwrecked heart
That noise that calls me from the dark
That noise that simply won't take flight
With the dawning of the morning light
As across the room the light it creeps
Towards that noise that often speaks to me

Christmas Party Man

It's Christmas, they all screamed

God bless us, everyone
All rushing to the dance floor
When that Wizard song came on

He wished it could be Christmas
Each and every day
He wished that the New Year
Would simply stay away

He danced upon the dance floor
Did dance like such a fool
And later had a drunken snog
With Carol from the typing pool

And come the witching hour sound
He was nowhere to be found
And he never made the restaurant
Got sick on beer and volovants

In Time

In time perhaps, we'll get it right
In time perhaps, we'll stop this fight
Call a truce
Demand a ceasefire
Be more loving in our desire
To make it work
And settle down to not-quite-bliss
We'll hold hands sometimes, kiss
And think back to more happy days
When that love we had was all the rage

The High Street

I remember the day the Woolworth's closed
Walking past it on the old high road
The staff all gathered round the pick n mix
Everything must go plastered on the Twix

And now it's Wilco's shutting down
Soon nothing left in this one-horse town
except betting shops and pay day loans
And those blokes that fix the stolen phones

Oh, what a town this used to be
Those childhood years, my mum and me
The vast array of sparkling shops
And the butcher with his sawdust chops

Each Saturday a Matchbox car
And a shank's pony walk so far
And an Action Man on Christmas Day
Until he deserted and ran away

Those days before Surprise, Surprise
Christmas Nights with Morcombe and Wise
And Fonzy and those Happy Days
And some kitchen-sink Play for Today

There's Nout Queer as Folk

There's this folk mob
At this pub I know
They take it all so serious
They never seem to slow

They're keeping up tradition
These songs of peasant land
They sing of merry England
That green and pleasant land

They sing of Cornish tin mines
And the Grimsby herring fleet
There's songs of revolution
And beheading's of the queen

They sing their songs in ernest
They dance a merry jig
And the landlord slips them something
Usually fifty quid

He thinks they're good for business
So there's really no alarm
And the punter's seem to like it
And they don't do any harm

But one thing he won't countenance
Is that bleeding Greensleeves song
Cos it causes so much nuisance
Especially when the footie's on!

The Snowman

All the children down our way
Sing songs about that fateful day
That terrible day last winter
Their snowman went away

Some say that he was kidnapped
Their parents they can't ask

All they know is what remained of him
His hat, his coat, his scarf

Some say he joined the army
And they sent him somewhere cold
Went off to fight for England
If the truth be sadly told

But what all those children don't know
And what all their parent's do
Is that the sun came out on Sunday
And he met his Waterloo

Some say he started sweating
And lost all of his weight
And then disappeared to nothing
And dripped under the garden gate

But those children loved that snowman
And they thought their hearts would break
Until one day come next winter
He suddenly came back again

I Blame it on that Song

You said you'd met another
Whilst in some restaurant
Now you say you love this other
Which I'm blaming on that song

Why can't you just stay with me
Why can't we just belong
Just why you do not love me
I blame it on that song

You heard it on the telly
One day when you were home
And you danced before the telly
Danced to that bleeding song

I claimed I'd never heard it
Yet you sing it all day long
You say you do swear by it
That stupid bleeding song

You said it's from a musical
On Broadway, oh, so long
But I've never even heard it
That stupid bleeding song

And now you've gone and left me
And now stands an empty bed
And now you've gone and left me
So I found my own song instead

One Night in L.A.

Let's recreate the ol' coral
This English boy in Southern Cal
with that sweet Laurel Canyon girl
As we dance the Santa Ana twirl

Like James Dean's ghost I come to you
This rebel boy without a clue
At Griffith Park Observatory
In La La Land you dance with me

Just like that Sundance kid called Jim

Strung out at the Hotel Morrison
Took that L.A. woman for a ride
Broke on through to the other side

Some troubadour with pompadour
And cosmic country blues to score
Eight miles high he took a trip
But ended up on Sunset Strip

In shades of Mrs Robinson
And Benjamin who's long-since gone
Heading north through Californ'
In search of Elaine Robinson

Those actors at the studio
Grown old now, with no place to go
save to their eternal resting plot
Valentino in some shady spot

Those freaks down at the Kit-Kat Club
Holding tight their ticket stub
As they dance beneath the killer moon
Like vampires at the Viper Room

And so I leave this strange old town
Of breathless heat, De Nero's frown
With Bowie's words accompanying
About that Twig-the-Wonder-Kid

Kitchen-Sink Dharma

I'm not sure I believe in God
Or the concept of God
Or any of his associates

I assume they all work
For the same corporation
I do believe though
In living the right way
Being nice to people
Not screwing people over
Treating people the way you'd
Like to be treated in return
Like the ten rules of Dharma
Or my own kitchen-sink version
In the hope of a happy life

One: Wake the same time every single day (6.00am for me)

Two: Tea, coffee, tea, coffee (repeat throughout the day)

Three: Try to do something nice for someone at least once a day (repeat)

Four: Dance in the kitchen (repeat)

Five: Play some David Bowie (repeat)

Six: Try throwing something away every day (save someone else having to do it, somewhere down the line, once you have gone)

Seven: Attempt doing something creative every day (repeat)

Eight: Kiss your dog (repeat)

Nine: Kiss your wife (repeat)

Ten: Play some David Bowie (repeat over and over again)

Dad

Daily I sat and watched you disappear
You in bed, me sat in that comfy chair
Disappear before my very eyes
Silence punctured by your heavy sighs
Your realization of that life no more
And me sat staring at that dirty floor
Yet every now and then you bathed in light
As long-term memories took flight
And you saw clearly once again
Reminisced those dear old friends
All of whom disappeared too
Despite brief spells that brought them back to you
Until just as quick they once again to fade
Disappearing in the evening shade
And you and I are back alone
And I can't help think how soon you'll go
Go away to who-knows-where
One day soon just disappear
And I'll be left to sit and stare
Sat there in that comfy chair

Sad Song

My embrace of song-writing was as surprising to me as the flood of poems that followed my inaugural effort on the verge of the pandemic. As with the poetry; as with the painting, which emerged at the same time, the song-writing came by way of my attempting to learn the piano, which had sat in our dining unused for more years than I can remember, and which had become the most expensive piece of 'furniture' we'd ever bought.

It was my wife, Sharon, that bought the piano, suddenly getting this urge, as is often the case with her, to start having piano lessons, coupled with a dreamy image, I think, of herself, come the next Christmas, entertaining us with a classical repertoire and a collection of Christmas classics. Not that I ever discouraged her from that dream – the whole point of the work I do with Open Book is to embrace both academia and creativity, regardless of any negative experience one may have had, education wise, in the past. However, I did have to point out to her that she might be better off just having a few lessons at first, to see if she liked it, and perhaps either buy or rent a cheap keyboard on which to practice, and then later, if she really took to it, make a proper investment in a piano of her own. Of course, my wife being my wife went straight off to Chapel's of Bond Street and immediately bought this beautiful electric Yamaha piano, which now takes pride of place in the dining room, and which, despite being unplayed and unloved ever since, sits majestically weighed down by a collection of clocks and photo frames and little figures of Tintin and Snowy, and the Peanuts crew of Charlie Brown, Lucy, Linus, Snoopy and Woodstock.

Not that I'm so much different from my wife. In fact, in accompaniment with that piano, our house contains an array of musical instruments from English concertinas to banjos, violins to electric guitars, penny whistles and harmonicas to acoustic guitars, all of which I had a 'good old go' at over the years, but none of which I ever mastered, especially the guitars, with my never being able to get my head around the concept of bar chords, let alone my fingers. Eventually I settled on the ukulele, which I mastered, if that's the right description, pretty quickly by way of repetition and my usual lazy approach of only attempting playing tunes that contained the dozen or so basic chords that I could easily play. Indeed, my strategy when it comes to anything creative is to completely ignore the traditional ways of learning and go immediately for a quick victory, even if I'll claim later that I was always more concerned with the spirit of folk/punk and that old adage of 'Three chords and the truth'!

And then one day during the lockdown I suddenly sat down at my wife's piano, lifted the lid, and simply started experimenting with a handful of white keys, before eventually moving on to learning a similar number of those chords that I'd been using to play songs of the ukulele and, using that same method of repetition. With my foot pressed firmly on the sustain pedal, I began playing around with all of these basic chords, especially some of the minor ones, which are usually quite sad, and discovered, in the process, that it produced a sweet, melancholy sound, and which definitely lent themselves to the kind of mood I usually find myself in. On top of that, for some bizarre reason, I discovered that the more I played I suddenly seemed to have adopted a not-quite-boogie-woogie style of playing, with most of my fingers moving in a very involuntary fashion, but which seemed to aid my style of playing and gave me a very unique sound, which was not quite jazz and not quite classical – people have since described it as 'Filmic', and have commented that much of the pieces that I compose (which sounds very grandiose) remind them of film soundtracks, which I'm always happy to take as a compliment.

Again, as with most things I do creatively, much of the progress I made was by of repetition – playing a song over and over again until I could do it without thinking, and then adding a new song each day or so following that, all of which I'd play over and over again until I'd built up quite a repertoire of songs that I could both play (on ukulele and piano) well enough and which gave me the confidence to sing along to also.

I think, what you need to remember is that this was at the very beginning of the lockdown when I found myself in the midst of this rich creative streak of form with my poetry writing, painting (with a flurry of paintings stacking up in my garden shed), with my ukulele playing, and now this form by way of the piano. So, it was probably not surprising that I suddenly found myself combining both the music and the poetry in the creation of a handful of songs, all of which appear here, including my very first effort – San Francisco Poet Song – which I truly believe is the best thing I've ever actually written, and which might surprise a lot of people, especially when considering I'd long since written a memoir, which has always been warmly received since its publication in 2014. Indeed, during the songs construction I can still remember playing that song over and over again during the course of an afternoon and my wife, who'd been sat listening to my playing in the other room, suddenly coming in and demanding to know whose song that was, and which is probably the greatest compliment she's ever paid me.

Enjoy!

Songs

All songs in this book are written and composed by Neil Bradley

San Francisco Poet Song

(C) these days, I find, (Em) I'm doing fine
(Dm) drunk most days on (F) heartbreak wine
(C) but one day I'll go to (Em) Californ'
(Dm) and sing this song (F) so forlorn

(C) bout climbing steps to old (Em) Coit Tower
(Dm) above the North Beach (F) witching hour
(C) and that pyramid cross (Em) Greenwich Street
(Dm) and Spec's Museum's (F) drunk retreat
(C) That trolley bus, the old (Em) F-Line
(Dm) those seals down at (F) Pier 39
(C) Those Fisherman down (Em) by the Wharf
(Dm) and sourdough (F) Boudin's, of course

(C) those waitresses (Em) who San Fran born
(Dm) that pour the coffee (F) early morn
(C) for all those poets (Em) of the Bay
(Dm) writing stanza's (F) all the day

(C) bout cable cars (Em) on Californ'
(Dm) that Ferry building (F) early morn
(C) to Alcatraz that (Em) and that great escape
(Dm) just across the Bay from (F) the Golden Gate
(C) and Giants at the (Em) old Ball Game
(Dm) lamenting runs by (F) Willie May
(C) when Buster posed (Em) then went away
(Dm) and Matt Cain pitched (F) that perfect game

(C) bout Dirty Harry (Em) Callaghan
(Dm) and Harvey and his (F) Castro plan
(C) who paid his premonition (Em) cost
(Dm) not just the camera shop (F) we lost

(C) and those rainbow kids (Em) who march with pride

(Dm) at the other end of (F) the MUNI ride

(C) so unaware of what (Em) went before

(Dm) all those 80s guys that (F) are no more

(C) those waitresses (Em) who San Fran born

(Dm) pour the coffee (F) early morn

(C) for all those poets (Em) of the Bay

(Dm) writing stanza's (F) all the day

(C) bout tie-dye kids on (Em) Ashbury

(Dm) that Haight Street counter (F) culture scene

(C) that summer that they (Em) promised Love

(Dm) and bombs were dropped (F) from far above

(C) and hopped aboard that (Em) Magic Bus

(Dm) and took a trip for all (F) of us

(C) till Charlie came and killed (Em) their dream

(Dm) that Helter Skelter family scene

(C) bout basking in (Em) the City Lights

(Dm) With Laureates on (F) Friday night

(C) and just across that (Em) alleyway

(Dm) to Vesuvio and those (F) drunken games

(C) and Kerouac tries to (Em) make amends

(Dm) raising glasses to (F) Absinth friends

(C) and Ginsberg screaming (Em) Howl's of pain

(Dm) all upon a (F) foggy day

(C) bout Miss Robinson and that (Em) strange affair

(Dm) and Benjamin that (F) followed there

(C) across that bridge (Em) across that Bay

(Dm) though traffic goes (F) the other way

(C) to Berkeley Hills on (Em) old BART trains

(Dm) with protest tears (F) and days of rage

(C) and Bears that match their (Em) yellow hue
(Dm) with coffee-house (F) piano blue

(C) the poet lays upon (Em) his bed
(Dm) dreaming of the (F) Grateful Dead
(C) across the room a book (Em) he throws
(Dm) and thinks he'll (F) take it On The Road

(C) walk down the hill and turn (Em) the bend
(Dm) to meet with dearest Nob Hill (F) friends
(C) who sit outside that closed (Em) café
(Dm) and lament another San Fran (F) day

(C) some days I think (Em) I won't go back
(Dm) just like my friend (F) the Zodiac
(C) and dream those dreams (Em) of Californ'
(Dm) just stay back home and (F) write this song

(C) bout waitresses, who (Em) San Fran born
(Dm) pour the coffee (F) early morn
(C) for poets of the (Em) 'Cisco Bay
(Dm) writing stanza's (F) every day
(C) before those dreams (Em) of Californ'
(Dm) before this song (F) so forlorn
(C) bout poets (Em) of the 'Cisco Bay
(Dm) those poets (F) and their rhyming ways
End on (C)

San Francisco Poets Song (additional verses)

Chorus

(C) those waitresses (Em) who San Fran born

(Dm) pour the coffee (F) early morn

(C) for all those poets (Em) of the Bay

(Dm) writing stanza's (F) all the day

(C) bout Neal Cassidy upon (Em) his bed

(Dm) dreaming of the (F) Grateful Dead

(C) across the room a book (Em) he throws

(Dm) and thinks he'll (F) take it On The Road

(C) with Big Chief Broom and Ken (Em) Kesey

(Dm) and crazy Jack the Mac (F) Murphy

(C) who once flew east, who once flew (Em) west

(Dm) who once flew over the cuckoo's (F) nest

(C) Devotees at that old (Em) Dead House

(Dm) those jeans we wore by (F) Levi Strauss

(C) to Chrissy Field sat by (Em) that fence

(Dm) that goofy stance of Hunter (F) Pence

(C) the sinking sand on Baker (Em) Beach

(Dm) that Golden Gate just out (F) of reach

(C) and those walks along the San Fran (Em) Bay

(Dm) where that girl with the ukulele (F) plays

Chorus

(C) bout breakfast down on (Em) old Sunset

(Dm) that old guy Chaz on the bus (F) we met

(C) Those Thai Chi folk who start (Em) their day

(Dm) in the park by Tony Bennett (F) way

(C) that Haight Street Army Surplus (Em) Store

(Dm) the Red Victorian not quite (F) next door

(C) those bathing boys in (Em) old Sutro

(Dm) those cheers for Marco (F) Scutero

(C) Bout sitting with my (Em) baby
(Dm) across the road from those (F) painted ladies
(C) the Airport at the Fillmore (Em) West
(Dm) and Grace Slick's pure white (F) rabbit test
(C) those Lindy-hoppers in the (Em) park
(Dm) that Seventies roller disco (F) dance
(C) and Maupin's tales of city (Em) life
(Dm) but avoid the Tenderloin (F) at night

Chorus

(C) Bout that Maltese Falcon (Em) Laundromat
(Dm) below Dashiell Hammett's (F) typing flat
(C) that pavilion at old (Em) Stow Lake
(Dm) in that park they call the (F) Golden Gate
(C) Bruce Bochy's tender (Em) grouchy smile
(Dm) Ferlinghetti's love for (F) Juan Marichal
(C) and that scenic trail from old (Em) Cliff House
(Dm) and that home to Walt and (F) and Micky Mouse

(C) Bout that Angel Island fog at (Em) dawn
(Dm) and that ferry cross to (F) Tiberon
(C) that museum with its Beat (Em) Collection
(Dm) Jack's Big Sur cabin (F) sad reflection
(C) and Tim Leary's call to you (Em) and me
(Dm) about the joys of (F) L.S.D.
(C) who beat a hasty love (Em) retreat
(Dm) tuned in, turned on (F) it was kinda' neat

Chorus

(C) Bout those steps on up to (Em) five-five-five

(Dm) on the California cable (F) ride

(C) even though that building wasn't (Em) there

(Dm) and despite that shot of (F) Fred Astaire

(C) little girl so blue, who went (Em) to heaven

(Dm) dying at the age of (F) twenty-seven

(C) and those angels at that (Em) speedway track

(Dm) and those Stones demand we (F) paint it black

(C) Twang Sunday at Thee (Em) old Parkside

(Dm) some Tiny Television (F) guitar slide

(C) where Lea Rose she laid (Em) her bones

(Dm) with California (F) country prose

(C) that Rothko painting (Em) orange-red

(Dm) that Love sign by the (F) flower bed

(C) where Steinbeck's Grapes of (Em) Wrath begins

(Dm) and those three World Series (F) title wins

My One True Masterpiece

(C) train was running late (F) today

(C) the same as it was (F) yesterday

(C) frustrating way to start the (F) day

(G7) 'cause it makes me late for (C) you

(C) today a nice museum (F) trip

(C) to get some oil painting (F) tips

(C) for one day when I get to (F) grips

(G7) and paint my master-(C)-piece

Chorus
(G) Oh, how the sun is (Am) shining

(F) on canvas pulled so (Dm) tight (E7)

(G) Oh, how the moon is (Am) beaming

(F) straight out from your (Dm) heart

(G) your heart (G7) heart

(C) those colours on the palette (F) knife

(C) those blues, those reds that fill the (F) sky

(C) my brush across the canvas (F) glides

(G7) as I paint my (C) masterpiece

(C) and in that room I'll leave to (F) dry

(C) that red and yellow sunset (F) sky

(C) and you will cast a tearful (F) eye

(G7) upon my (C) masterpiece

Chorus

(C) been thinking somewhere down the (F) line

(C) with you perhaps to share my (F) time

(C) and we will live that painter's (F) life

(G7) 'neath Vincent's starry (C) night

(C) and you'll stand back and you'll (F) admire

(C) those colours that refuse to (F) dry

(C) and you will see my painter's (F) eye

(G7) as it falls upon your (C) face

Chorus

(C) and I will take your hand in (F) mine

(C) and we'll walk through the rest of (F) life

(C) two muses to the painter's (F) eye

(G7) that life a (C) masterpiece

(C) and we will live a happy (F) life

(C) avoid that Vincent painter's (F) strife

(C) straight to those starry, starry (F) nights

(G7) that I will spend with (C) you

Chorus

(C) and you'll be in the forefront (F) still

(C) I hope to God you say you (F) will

(C) and I will paint the waters (F) still

(G7) with skies so void of (C) grey

(C) and that girl upon the canvas (F) there

(C) with pretty eyes, that pretty (F) stare

(C) and I will love you then and (F) there

(G7) and each and every (C) day

Chorus

(C) and when it's time to clean my (F) brush

(C) with turpentine, so it don't (F) rust

(C) my masterpiece we will (F) discuss

(G7) before hanging on the (C) wall

(C) and then we'll sit beneath that (F) sky

(C) so void of grey we'll almost (F) cry

(C) your pretty face you'll try to (F) hide

(G7) God's one true (C) masterpiece

Chorus

(C) now sitting in the evening (F) shade

(C) and all my colours start to (F) fade

(C) memories they fall on happy (F) days

(G7) those days I spent with (C) you

(C) just walking round that (F) gallery

(C) that day I said please marry (F) me

(C) and you became my (F) destiny

(G7) my one true (C) masterpiece

Chorus

(C) and in that gallery (F) somewhere

(C) the people they will gather (F) there

(C) and all of them will stop and (F) stare

(G7) at that painted (C) masterpiece

(C) and some will cast a tearful (F) eye

(C) upon that red and yellow (F) sky

(C) the two of us though (F) long-since died

(G7) living in that (C) masterpiece

Chorus (to fade)

My Life (written for piano)

(Left Hand – Dm/Right Hand – C)

(Dm/C) Some days I can't get out of bed
(Dm/C) too many troubles in my head
(C/C) My life, my life

(Dm/C) 'cause when I think about the this and that
(Dm/C) I know that none of it is coming back
(C/C) My life, my life

(Dm/C) Because it happened all those times before
(Dm/C) looking back at all those closing doors
(C/C) My life, my life

(Dm/C) those loves I had they didn't last
(Dm/C) and those that did, you know, they went too fast
(C/C) My life, my life

(Dm/C) Now (Em/C) Then (G/C) Old (F/C) Friends

(Dm/C) people tell me don't be looking back
(Dm/C) 'cause I can't change none of that
(C/C) My life, my life

(Dm/C) and when I sit there and I think of that
(Dm/C) you know I really can't help feeling bad
(C/C) My life, my life

(Dm/C) sometimes it's good, sometimes it's bad
(Dm/C) but that don't change a single fact
(C/C) My life, my life

(Dm/C) now each new morning when I go to bat
(Dm/C) my mind's already thinking 'bout the catch
(C/C) My life, my life

(Dm/C) Now (Em/C) Then (G/C) Old (F/C) Friends

(Dm/C) I saw a girl once and she smiled at me
(Dm/C) but that was on some other street
(C/C) My life, my life

(Dm/C) I used to look up at the stars at night
(Dm/C) but through the clouds they never seemed so bright
(C/C) My life, my life

(Dm/C) Some days I wonder what it's all about
(Dm/C) how I could scream, how I could shout
(C/C) My life, my life

(Dm/C) but then that feeling, well, it goes away
(Dm/C) just comes back to me another day
(C/C) My life, my life

(Dm/C) Now (Em/C) Then (G/C) Old (F/C) Friends

(Dm/C) and when I think back to those lonely nights
(Dm/C) I think I may as well give up the fight
(C/C) My life, my life

(Dm/C) because this life, you know, it's so damn hard
(Dm/C) leaves me thinking that I feel so tired
(C/C) My life, my life

(Dm/C) and now I know that if it weren't for you
(Dm/C) that life before, it would be through

(C/C) My life, my life

(Dm/C) 'cause when you smiled at me the sun shone through
(Dm/C) to think this life was not so cruel
(C/C) My life, my life

(Dm/C) Now (Em/C) Then (G/C) Old (F/C) Friends
(Dm/C) Now (Em/C) Then (G/C) Old (F/C) Friends

A Love Divine

(Am) I met a girl long time ago

(F) and we went through the to-and-fro

(C) of teenage love then not so young

(G) don't know now when it begun

(Am) she led me down the garden path

(F) those days I thought our love would last

(C) when it's awful swell, it's awful great

(G) she kisses me, I reciprocate

Dm/F/C – Dm/F/C/G

(Am) until heart-broke and real lonesome

(F) filled with pain – just like this song

(C) no longer drunk on sweetheart wine

(G) now just drunk most of the time

(Am) so full of pain and such regret

(F) for that girl I can't forget

(C) who went with me out on the run

(G) don't know now when it begun

Dm/F/C – Dm/F/C/G

(Am) she came to me from outa' town

(F) and all those times we'd fool around

(C) some nights we slept without a sound

(G) just our breathing in and breathing out

(Am) until, one day, she stopped to breath

(F) and she just upped and took her leave

(C) leaving me real high and dry

(G) I'm sorry, Babe, I gotta' fly

Dm/F/C – Dm/F/C/G

(Am) this love is meant for someone else

(F) leaving me upon the shelf

(C) of love divine and no regret

(G) I lost the best I'd ever get

(Am) now, if you see her on the street

(F) a girl, someday, you might well meet

(C) just stop a while and think of me

(G) of my sad life turned history

Dm/F/C – Dm/F/C/G

(Am) 'cause she'll steal your heart like she stole mine

(F) that love you thought was so divine

(C) will start to fade behind the light

(G) just when you think you're doing fine

(Am) 'cause she'll lead you down that garden path

(F) of love divine that will not last

(C) till you stop a while and ask yourself

(G) about that boy left on the shelf

Dm/F/C – Dm/F/C/G

(Am) if you meet that girl with starry eyes

(F) don't let her take you by surprise

(C) oh, she'll steal your heart one cloudless night

(G) and the moon will blind your foolish eyes

(Am) 'cause she can't love, least not for long

(F) and soon enough she's movin' on

(C) off to some or other place

(G) where those breathing nights will soon take place

Dm/F/C – Dm/F/C/G

(Am) with someone else, some other town

(F) and she don't want you hangin' round

(C) 'cause she's a heart that's made of steel

(G) and your sweet heart she's bound to steal

(Am) like she did mine, that love divine

(F) I guess it happens all the time

(C) to guys like me, to guys like you

(G) I'm sorry, Babe, I guess we're through

Dm/F/C – Dm/F/C/G

(Am) until the memories start to fade

(F) your life with her some big charade

(C) just like mine those years ago

(G) once we'd been through the to-and-fro

(C) until you can't remember when

(G) that girl who came and went again

(Am) until you can't remember why

(F) that love divine began to die

Dm/F/C – Dm/F/C/G - Am/F/C/G - Dm/F/C – Dm/F/C/G

Repeat to Fade

I'm A Good Ol' Country Boy

(C) Now, I'm gonna' go to Nashville (F)

(G7) fake a country (C) song

(C) move right into Cashville (F)

(G7) come on Country (C) strong

(AM) gonna' summon Hank's old (F) spirit

(G7) write an Opry (C) tune

(C) gonna' have a big (F) hit

(G7) live my life to (C) ruin

Chorus

(C) Now, I'm a good ol' country (F) boy

(G7) I really ain't that bad (C)

(C) a good old-fashioned country (F) boy

(G7) I get that from my (C) dad

(AM) my cowboy boots are rattle (F) snake

(G7) my buckle's real turquoise (C)

(C) and when I play the honky (F) tonks

(G7) I really make some noise (C)

(C) Now, I'm gonna' hop a freight (F) train

(G7) just like the hobbo's (C) do

(C) roll right into Nashville (F)

(G7) sing a country (C) tune

(AM) and when I stroll down (F) Broadway

(G7) my bolo pulled up (C) tight

(C) I'll find the nearest honky (F) tonk

(G7) and sing some Patsy (C) Cline

Chorus

(C) Now, I'm gonna' buy a (F) pick-up

(G7) drive right into (C) town

(C) ain't gonna' make no (F) slip-up

(G7) I'll tear this country(C) down

(AM) I'm gonna' fly the big (F) flag

(G7) know just what to (C) do

(C) gonna' form a jug (F) band

(G7) that red, that white, that (C) blue

Chorus

(C) Sunday mornin', comin' (F) down

(G7) I 'm gonna' dress in (C) black

(C) just like that bird out on the (F) wire

(G7) I'll sing some Johnny (C) Cash

(AM) I'm gonna' sing with real (F) desire

(G7) Just like that boy named (C) Sue

(C) Play that burning ring of (F) fire

(G7) and sing a song for (C) you

(C) Now, if you're a good ol' country (F) boy

(G7) and you really ain't that bad (C)

(C) if you're a good old-fashioned country (F) boy

(G7) and you get that from your (C) dad

(AM) if your cowboy boots are rattle (F) snake

(G7) and your buckle's real turquoise (C)

(C) then come and join this fiddle (F) band

(G7) and make some god'damn' (C) noise!

Repeat Chorus to fade

Be With Me

Intro: D-A-C-G

(Bm) I'd see you some days on the (Am) street

(Bm) those days I'd orchestrate (Am) our meet

(Bm) you thought it (Am) serendipity

(Bm) those days I'd stalk you in my (Am) dream

Chorus x 2

(D) Be with me

(A) Kiss me

(C) Hold Me

(G) Love me

(Bm) there was a time when I was not (Am) like this

(Bm) in summer's rain and winter's (Am) kiss

(Bm) those days of pain and (Am) equal bliss

(Bm) that life I thought we wouldn't (Am) miss

Chorus

(Bm) that thing we had that went (Am) away

(Bm) you couldn't bring yourself to (Am) stay

(Bm) you came and went some rainy (Am) day

(Bm) Your mind I truly couldn't (Am) sway

Chorus

(Bm) I just can't give you (Am) anything

(Bm) that song we had, you never (Am) sing

(Bm) as the cold of winter (Am) comes again

(Bm) you say it doesn't mean a (Am) thing

Chorus x 2 – end on (D)

It's a Shame

(C) I'm trying hard to live my (F) life

(C) The way you always (F) said

(C) The way you always (F) did

It's a (G) shame

(C) but I find it hard to live that (F) way

(C) when clouds form on a rainy (F) day

(C) when I haven't got a thing to (F) say

It's a (G) shame (G7)

(C) I'm trying hard to figure (F) out

(C) those things that made you scream and (F) shout

(C) just why we couldn't work it (F) out

It's a (G) shame

(C) and now it seems so long (F) ago

(C) the way it went I just don't (F) know

(C) that we went through the to and (F) fro

It's a (G) shame (G7)

Chorus

(C) it's a shame this thing that we once (F) had

(C) how soon it soured and turned (F) bad

(Dm) those days of love

(E7) we knew they wouldn't (Am) last

(C) it's a shame the way it died so (F) soon

(C) didn't even last the (F) afternoon

(Dm) those days of love

(E7) they ended all so (Am) fast

(F) how those days of love (G) they ended all so (C) fast

(C) I wish you would come back to (F) me

(C) I wish you'd sometimes think of (F) me

(C) I wish you'd sometimes call to (F) me

It's a (G) shame

(C) but your heart it's with another (F) love

(C) whilst mine is lost in clouds (F) above

(C) sometimes I think I've had (F) enough

It's a (G) shame (G7)

(C) and now it's so late in the (F) day

(C) cause the morning's when you went (F) away

(C) won't come back to me another (F) day

It's a (G) shame

(C) those cigarettes and cheap-store (F) wine

(C) those grapes that withered on the (F) vine

(C) you know, we never had the (F) time

It's a (G) shame (G7)

Chorus

(C) looking back now on my (F) life

(C) that love we had was so (F) divine

(C) perhaps we didn't give it (F) time

It's a (G) shame

(C) but that was many years (F) ago

(C) just how I lost you, I don't (F) know

(C) in the end, I guess, I was too (F) slow

It's a (G) shame (G7)

(C) walking down this lonely (F) road

(C) without no sense of where to (F) go

(C) just walking long and feeling (F) old

It's a (G) shame

(C) and now the night it falls on (F) me

(C) those clouds so dark they blanket (F) me

(C) you folks, I'll tell you this for (F) free

It's a (G) shame (G7) - *Repeat chorus to fade*

My Mother's Love

(C) As I walk on up this road (G) ahead

(Am) these words are forming in my (F) head

(C) I think I'll turn these (G) words into a song (Am) – (F)

(C) I think I'll turn these (G) words into a song (C)

(C) 'neath iridescent clouds (G) above

(Am) I'm thinking 'bout my mother's (F) love

(C) those childhood dreams (G) they didn't seem to last (Am) – (F)

(C) those childhood dreams (G) they didn't seem to last (C)

(C) and now my life has gone (G) nowhere

(Am) my mother's in the ground (F) somewhere

(C) though her love for me (G) it reaches way on past (Am) – (F)

(C) though her love for me (G) it reaches way on past (C)

(C) and the only thing I'm certain (G) of

(Am) beneath that galaxy (F) above

(C) my mother's love (G) will get me to the end (Am) – (F)

(C) my mother's love (G) will get me to the end (C)

(C) and as I walk down this lonely (G) road

(Am) I'm feelin' very much (F) alone

(C) don't even have a dog (G) to call my friend (Am) – (F)

(C) don't even have a dog (G) to call my friend (C)

(C) yet my life it wasn't always (G) so

(Am) though the happiness it come and (F) go

(C) not sure it's coming (G) back to me again (Am) – (F)

(C) not sure it's coming (G) back to me again (C)

(C) those childhood dreams seemed always (G) near

(Am) even though they've gone for good (F) I fear

(C) am I foolish still (G) to want those dreams again? (Am) – (F)

(C) am I foolish still (G) to want those dreams again? (C)

(C) and as the sun machine makes it's (G) descent

(Am) and my journey seems so near its (F) end

(C) the future seems to (G) offer little more (Am) – (F)

(C) the future seems to (G) offer little more (C)

(C) still, I think I'll go on round the (G) bend

(Am) in the hope I'll meet some loving (F) friend

(C) is that too much to ask (G) of you, my Lord? (Am) – (F)

(C) is that too much to ask (G) of you, my Lord? (C)

(C) until they put me in the (G) ground

(Am) like my mother in some other (F) town

(C) years left to me with them (G) I vow to spend (Am) – (F)

(C) years left to me with them (G) I vow to spend (C)

(C) and they will grieve just like they (G) must

(Am) as my childhood dream's they turn to (F) dust

(C) and nature starts it (G) all over again (Am) – (F)

(C) and nature starts it (G) all over again (C)

(C) and I come back as some other (G) man

(Am) the beauty of my sweet Lord's (F) plan

(C) even though I stopped (G) believing long ago (Am) – (F)

(C) even though I stopped (G) believing long ago (C)

(C) now as I sing this song my (G) friend

(Am) I'm walking down that road (F) again

(C) I hope it didn't (G) trouble you so bad (Am) – (F)

(C) I hope it didn't (G) trouble you so bad (C)

(C) 'cause this song I sing for every (G) man

(Am) about the beauty of God's (F) plan

(C) and that mother's love (G) that guides me to my last (Am) – (F)

(C) that mother's love (G) that guides me to the last (C)

Shabby Man

(C) Sometimes you'll see him walking on the (G) street (G7)

(E7) He's a bloke, you might well sometimes (AM) meet

(C) You'll see him raise his hat as if to (G) greet (G7)

(F) He's a shabby man (G) unsteady of his (C) feet

(C) Years ago he worked for the (G) G.P.O. (G7)

(E7) got sacked for calling his boss a (AM) so-and-so

(C) 'cause he's the type who wouldn't let it (G) go (G7)

(F) and in the end (G) they told him where to (C) go

(C) These days he just can't earn an honest (G) bob (G7)

(E7) so now most days you'll find him on the (AM) rob

(C) and he saves up all his loot for a rainy (G) day (G7)

(F) two weeks in Margate (G) in the early (C) May

Chorus

(C) he's a shabby man, he has his shabby (G) ways (G7)

(E7) and his shabby coat has seen much better (AM) days

(C) and his shabby hat is crumpled on his (G) head (G7)

(F) and in winter time (G) he wears it all in (C) bed

(C) now Saturday's he goes to (G) Sainsbury's (G7)

(E7) and gives all of the produce there a (AM) squeeze

(C) grabs milk and bread and a box of (G) Coco-Pops (G7)

(F) stuffs them in his coat (G) and nicks the bleedin' (C) lot

(C) Most people think his name might well be (G) Fred (G7)

(E7) 'cause he looks like he has just got out of (AM) bed

(C) and when he does he makes a cup of (G) tea (G7)

(F) cause his routines really (G) just like you and (C) Me

(C) most nights you'll find him sitting in the (G) pub (G7)

(E7) takes off his shoes and gives his feet a (AM) rub

(C) most nights he can be trusted to (G) behave (G7)

(F) and when he leaves (G) he gives them all a (C) wave

Chorus

(C) Now in the war they sent him (G) overseas (G7)

(E7) but he got shot whilst landing on the (AM) beach

(C) now every year he limps past the (G) Cenotaph (G7)

(F) and thinks of all those comrades (G) from his (C) past

(C) he had a wife, but she died long (G) ago (G7)

(E7) and every year he cries for his dear old (AM) Flo

(C) and on that day he even has a (G) shave (G7)

(F) puts fresh-cut flowers (G) on his poor Flo's (C) grave

(C) Now he's the kind of melancholy (G) type (G7)

(E7) most days you'll find him contemplating (AM) life

(C) the truth is that, deep down, he's really (G) sad (G7)

(F) yet most assume (G) he's simply bleedin' (C) mad

Chorus

(C) now he's got a little dog he calls his (G) mate (G7)

(E7) you'll often see them at the garden (AM) gate

(C) oh, he loves that dog and he walks him every (G) day (G7)

(F) oh, he walks that (G) dog, even when it (C) rains

(C) now some day's he will smoke a fag or (G) two (G7)

(E7) especially on those days he's feelin' (AM) blue

(C) no soon he stubs it out he has a (G) cough (G7)

(F) but then he lights (G) another and he's (C) off

(C) now he's got his memories but most are (G) sad (G7)

(E7) but thinking of his wife it makes him (AM) glad

(C) cause as man and wife they really were a (G) match (G7)

(F) till cancer brought (G) that cursed, bleedin' (C) catch

(C) so if you see him walking down your (G) street (G7)

(E7) please raise your hat and give him smile to (AM) greet

(C) 'cause he's really not as bad as people (G) say (G7)

(F) He's a shabby man (G) who lives that shabby (C) way

Repeat Chorus to Fade

The Old Guitar Picker

(C) T'was in some bar in (G7) Richmond

(F) North Carolina (C) way

A man sat on a (G7) barstool

(F) and sang the blues (C) away

(C) Oh, he sang 'em all the sad (G7) tunes

(F) in his (C) repertoire

Oh, he just kept right on (G7) picking

(F) at that old (C) guitar

Chorus

(F) But the people they (C) ignored him

(F) too busy drinking (C) wine

(F) And beer and thunder (C) whisky

(G7) paid him no never (C) mind

(F) Oh, they didn't hear the (C) words he sang

(F) or hear his sad (C) refrain

(F) They just kept right on (C) drinking

(G7) those lonesome songs in (C) vain

(C) But that man he picked his (G7) guitar

(F) though they took him for a (C) fool

Sang songs about the (G7) Southland

(F) all the evening (C) through

And that evening when he'd (G7) finished

(F) tipped his hat to no (C) applause

Picked up that battered (G7) guitar

(F) and headed for the (C) door

Chorus

(C) that night he wrote a new (G7) song

(F) and put it to a (F) tune

Bout some lonely guitar (G7) player

(F) who sang in some (C) saloon

Next day he grabbed his (G7) guitar

(F) and headed back to (C) town

To sing for all those lonely (G7) folk

 (F) he wouldn't let 'em (C) down

Chorus (to fade)

The Girl with Auburn Hair

(C) One day upon a long a country (G) mile

(F) I met a maiden (C) fare

(C) She stopped a ways and smiled at (G) me

(F) The girl with auburn (C) hair

(C) I said to her where do you (G) roam

(F) On this cold, sunny (C) day

(C) She said in search of her true (G) love

(F) Who's left and gone (C) away

(F) who's left (G) and gone (C) away

(C) I wondered if she'd search for (G) me

(F) If her true love I'd (C) be

(C) She said I'm welcome to walk a (G) ways

(F) In her sad comp-(C)-any

(C) So, down the road we wander-(G)-ed

(F) With no real end in (C) sight

(C) No vision of her one true (G) love

(F) further down the road did (C) spy

(F) Further (G) down the road (C) did spy

(C) Her lonely eyes looked on the (G) ground

(F) For footprints in the (C) dust

(C) But the only footprints were (G) behind

(F) And those were hers and mine, (C) and mine

(C) I told her stop her wander-(G)-ng

(F) Her one true love has (C) gone

(C) I picked some sad guitar for (G) her

(F) And sang a lonesome (C) song

(F) and I sang (G) a lonesome (C) song

(C) Along the ways she took my (G) hand

(F) in mine it did (C) belong

(C) as we walked along in silent (G) pose

(F) I thought about this (C) song

(C) I thought about the words I'd (G) use

(F) if this old song I'd (C) share

(C) and whistled a sweet (G) melody

(F) to the girl with auburn (C) hair

(F) to the girl (G) with auburn (C) hair

(C) as we walked 'neath the sky so (G) blue

(F) with heaven far (C) above

(C) the clouds were disappear-(G)-ing

(F) just like her one true (C) love

(C) I stole a glimpse at her sweet (G) face

(F) her womanhood in (C) bloom

(C) the dress she wore of linen (G) lace

(F) constructing this here (C) tune

(F) constructing (G) this here (C) tune

(C) how far we walked upon that (G) day

(F) I really couldn't (C) tell

(C) it seemed to me a life-(G)-time

(F) yet was no time at (C) all

(C) and when the sun began to (G) set

(F) upon that country (C) plane

(C) I kissed the maid with my all my (G) heart

(F) then kissed her once (C) again

(F) then kissed G) her once (C) again

(C) and now I sing this song to (G) you

(F) this song I wrote for (C) her

(C) that sweet young maid upon the (G) road

(F) the girl with auburn (C) hair

(C) the girl who stole my heart (G) away

(F) whilst seeking one that's (C) lost

(C) the one she called her one true (G) love

(F) the one who double-(C)-crossed

(F) the one (G) who double-(C)-crossed

(C) I asked her to turn back (G) again

(F) To go the other (C) way

(C) To walk with me my (G) destiny

(F) Upon that lonesome (C) day

(C) I asked her if she'd marry (G) me

(F) To her devote my (C) care

(C) And I would be her one true (G) love

(F) that girl with auburn (C) hair

(F) that girl (G) with auburn (C) hair

That Man from Memphis

(C) I met a man in (G) Memphis
(F) a real long time (C) ago
(C) he told me all bout (G) Elvis
(F) and that Devil (C) Rock n Roll
(C) he taught me how to (G) Country
(F) a little Western (C) too
(C) taught me how to write a (G) song
(F) and sing it with the (C) Blues

Chorus
(G) oh, give me a home where the (C) cool whisky flows
(G) and I wake with a pain in my (D) head
(G) there's a man dressed in black
(C) a black coat, a black hat
(G) and he's demanding (D) I pay up my (G) debt

(C) but recent that man (G) lonesome
(F) and old beyond his (C) years
(C) succumbed to drinking (G) whisky
(F) and for him I shed a (C) tear
(C) passing in some lonesome (G) room
(F) nobody at his (C) call
(C) died listening to the (G) radio
(F) and that Devil (C) Rock n Roll

Chorus

(C) and now when I play (G) Country
(F) that man comes to my (C) head
(C) And I think about his (G) dying
(F) in that lonesome (C) bed
(C) that man I met in (G) Memphis

(F) a real long time (C) ago

(C) who taught me all bout (G) Elvis

(F) and that Devil (C) rock n roll

Chorus (to fade)

If you see Sid, tell him

(C) his wife she became poorly (G) the doctor's thought it for the best
(Am) and so he gripped her hand gently (F) as she took her final rest
(C) and as she went up to heaven (G) he sobbed and he did cry
(Am) because his dear departed wife (F) had gone right off and died

(C) Back home he drew the curtains (G) and then switched on the gas
(Am) put a shilling in the meter (F) and prayed so for the best
(C) but the board had cut his gas off (G) just the week before
(Am) so he got back to his feet again (F) and slammed the oven door

(C) Oh, why did God take her? (G) He really didn't know
(Am) He should've took him instead, (F) and not his dear old Flo
(C) but life it isn't always fair (G) and death is just as bad
(Am) and so he sat and cursed the gas board (F) and he lit another fag

(C) but just then they put the gas back on (G) as he engaged the match
(Am) and as he took one big old drag (F) he knew there was a catch
(C) and as he took another drag (G) the cooker it came on
(Am) that cigarette it killed him (F) he was blown to kingdom come

(C) Now if you're feeling lonely (G) just think of poor old Sid
(Am) As Flo, she dear departed (F) just think of what he did
(C) He looked towards the gas board (G) his heart for them to mend
(Am) but it was the fags that killed him (F) what done him in the end

(C) he should've gone electric (G) or bought some shares instead
(Am) or when Flo, she dear departed (F) just taken to his bed
(C) He should've cut the fags out (G) all those years ago
(Am) cause the cigarettes'll kill ya' (F) just like they did poor Flo

C) and now it's heaven where he loves her (G) just as he did on earth
(Am) and now you can tell the gas board (F) Sid leaves them with this curse

(C) there are no shilling meters (G) in that sky above

(Am) and there is no bleedin' gas board (F) to rob you of your love

(C) Now the moral of the story (G) is pay your bills on time

(Am) but when Maggie sold the gas off (F) it was a bleedin' crime

(C) because the privatised are heartless (G) and they just want their dough

(Am) so if you see Sid tell him (F) and warn him 'bout poor Flo

No Money Back

Intro: C-Em7-Am-F-Fm7

(C) I came back to the (Em7) house one day

(Am) It seemed as if (F) you'd gone away

(C) Gone away to (Em7) who-knows-where

(Am) It seemed as if (F) you didn't care

(C) No message for me (Em7) left in kind

(Am) It seemed as if I'd (F) slipped your mind

(C) There's boxes in (Em7) the other room

(Am) Discarded in the (F) morning gloom

(C) Those hangers in (Em7) the wardrobe there

(Am) Those shoes you left (F) atop the stairs

(C) Your dressing gown's (Em7) still hanging there

(Am) Your things I'm (F) finding everywhere

C-G-C-F-C

C-G-Am-F-Fm7

Chorus

(C) Don't let it go this (Em7) thing we had

(Am) Just remember there's no (F) money back

(C) No guarantees, no (Em7) promise notes

(Am) Just two lost souls in (F) our winter coats

(C) Stood on that beach as the(Em7) tide came in

(Am) Those crashing waves wash (F) away our sins

(C) Of love that was of (Em7) love that's been

(Am) Those fights we had those(F) stupid things

(C) Those silent breaths on (Em7) the telephone

(Am) That message, sorry, (F) no one's home

(C) So, don't let it go this (Em7) thing we had

(Am) Just remember there's no (F) money back

C-G-C-F-C

C-G-Am-F-Fm7

Chorus

C-G-C-F-C

C-G-Am-F-Fm7

(C) Your love is like some (Em7) TV show

(Am) I re-mem-ber from (F) years ago

(C) Still waiting for some (Em7) old repeat

(Am) For you to walk back (F) down this street

(C) To knock upon that old (Em7) street door

(Am) Just down from (F) number forty-four

(C) Canned laughter in (Em7) the afternoon

(Am) To cheer away that (F) morning gloom

(C) When suddenly those (Em7) words come back

(Am) Words to that old (F) familiar track

(C) That song I played it (Em7) on repeat

(Am) And gently moved my (F) shuffling feet

C-G-C-F-C

C-G-Am-F-Fm7

Chorus

C-G-C-F-C

C-G-Am-F-Fm7

(C) I can't forget that (Em7) time we had

(Am) That life we had (F) those days way back

(C) When everything was (Em7) morning sun

(Am) When love, it seemed, (F) had just begun

(C) Those days when we had (Em7) not a care

(Am) The two of us (F) just standing there

(C) With both of us in (Em7) lover's vibe

(Am) Those days now I (F) just can't describe

(C) Those days when we had (Em7) much to gain

(Am) Our love not quite yet (F) down the drain

(C) Until all of that (Em7) pain set in
(Am) Until we lost (F) that loving thing

C-G-C-F-C
C-G-Am-F-Fm7
Chorus
C-G-C-F-C
C-G-Am-F-Fm7

(C) To me you were no (Em7) passing fad
(Am) The two of us (F) were both as bad
(C) To kill it slowly (Em7) from the start
(Am) Set out to break (F) each other's heart
(C) Yet in-between we (Em7) danced along
(Am) Dancing to some (F) morning song
(C) In love for real (Em7) if for a time
(Am) That love we had (F) our only crime
(C) until that day you (Em7) end it all
(Am) And now you won't (F) return my call
(C) To give it up (Em7) the way you did
(Am) Yet in my heart (F) I still forgive

C-G-C-F-C
C-G-Am-F-Fm7
Chorus
C-G-C-F-C
C-G-Am-F-Fm7

(C) Thinking back that (Em7) life we had
(Am) Those memories come (F) flooding back
(C) Drowning me beneath (Em7) the waves
(Am) Robbing me those (F) carefree days
(C) Those days I spent with (Em7) you back then
(Am) My one true love (F) my one true friend

(C) You beneath the (Em7) eiderdown

(Am) And me sat in my (F) dressing gown

(C) That world outside (Em7) we blocked it out

(Am) Left we two in (F) no real doubt

(C) To simply waste the (Em7) days away

(Am) Deterred by early (F) morning rain

C-G-C-F-C

C-G-Am-F-Fm7

Chorus

C-G-C-F-C

C-G-Am-F-Fm7

(C) That song we danced (Em7) to years ago

(Am) That song we danced to (F) nice and slow

(C) We two beneath (Em7) the mirror ball

(Am) For love in wait (F) for us to fall

(C) And now the music's (Em7) finally stopped

(Am) And all I hear's (F) that ticking clock

(C) That clicks away (Em7) to my demise

(Am) That clicks away (F) to our goodbyes

(C) And now I think about it (Em7) far too much

(Am) That singer wasn't (F) up to much

(C) I think about it far (Em7) too long

(Am) He didn't even (F) know our song

C-G-C-F-C

C-G-Am-F-Fm7

Repeat Chorus to fade

Open Book

Goldsmiths Open Book aims to break down the barriers that discourage people from entering Higher Education. Open Book works closely with a network of agencies to support people form a wide range of backgrounds, including those on the margins of society, those with a negative experience of the Criminal Justice system, those from an addiction background and/or with previous mental health issues, those who are homeless, those in challenging caring roles, as well as those from traditional working class backgrounds, who have never truly considered Further and Higher Education as any kind of route to enhancing their future life choices.

Open Book, whilst modestly funded by Goldsmiths, University of London, relies heavily on charitable donation, which funds an array of academic and creative projects, with positively life-changing outcomes – including for myself.

If you would like to make a donation, or would like further information on the invaluable work Open Book does, please contact us at:

Open Book
Goldsmiths, University of London
New Cross, London
SE14 6NW

openbookadmin@gold.ac.uk

More by this Author

Four Funerals and a Wedding (Journeys in Creative and Life Writing)

Available from Amazon/Kindle Direct Publishing

"My intention had always been to write a novel, yet, almost by accident, I ended up writing this instead!"

In his first book the author struggles to write a novel, which accidently results in him writing a memoir about the loss of four prominent family members, but which includes novel extracts, life writing exercises, and his thoughts on what it is to be a writer.

In the Pipeline

The £25.00 Dog

The follow-up memoir to *Four Funerals and Wedding - Journeys in Creative and Life Writing,* which continues on from where that inaugural memoir ends.

My Dead Girlfriend

The story of a washed-up writer, who idles his days away in a coffee shop at the top of a hill in San Francisco.

The Brass Angel Trilogy

The debut novel, plus its two follow-up novels, none of which the author has had the heart or the energy to finish.

Printed in Dunstable, United Kingdom